Me and
My Boats

iUniverse, Inc.
New York   Bloomington

iUniverse books may be ordered through booksellers or by contacting:

iUniverse
1663 Liberty Drive
Bloomington, IN 47403
www.iuniverse.com
1-800-Authors (1-800-288-4677)

ISBN: 978-1-4401-5625-0 (sc)
ISBN: 978-1-4401-5626-7 (ebook)

Printed in the United States of America

iUniverse rev. date: 8/5/2009

Me and My Boats

Parker W. Hirtle

Parker and Joyce Sailing on Buzzards Bay

Introduction and Dedication

This book is the story of my life with boats, spanning a time period of about 70 years. It starts with a rowboat on the LaHave River in Nova Scotia and ends with the sale of our last cruising sailboat, a Crealock 37. Most of the book is about our cruising adventures on the New England coast, especially Maine. Included are descriptions, plans, and photographs of the cruising boats we purchased and the dinghies and small boats I made or bought, and in some cases designed. There are many photographs and simple charts indicating some of the harbors and anchorages visited and the courses followed.

The title of the book is somewhat of a misnomer, since my wife Joyce was co-owner of several of the boats in the book. She also was my first mate, sailed with me for almost 40 years, and supported me through fair weather and foul – but I was the one who got us seriously into boating and cruising when I bought the Alacrity, a little British "pocket cruiser".

Joyce made copious notes in the logbooks of all our boats except for the Alacrity. Much of the information in this book comes from the logbooks, supplemented by my memory and photographs taken during our cruising years. Without Joyce's copious notes and support the book could not have been written.

Having been born in Nova Scotia, the love of boats and boating was in my blood from the beginning. Perhaps the same may be said for Joyce, whose family came from Newfoundland, a seafaring area similar in many ways to Nova Scotia. Maybe this is why she was such a willing participant in our boating adventures.

The book is dedicated with love to my dear shipmate Joyce.

Parker W. Hirtle
Lexington, Massachusetts
2009

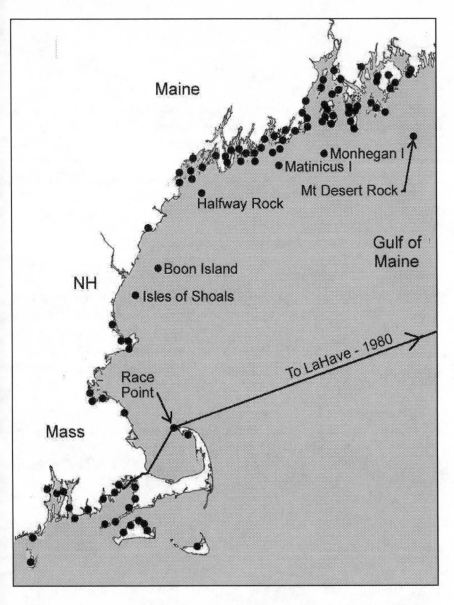

Cruising Grounds

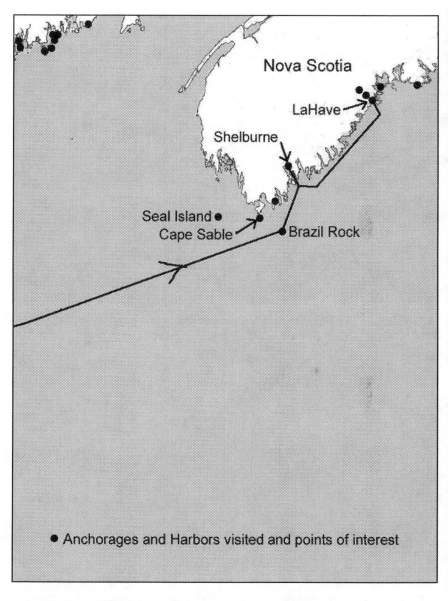

Nova Scotia

LaHave

Shelburne

Seal Island ●
Cape Sable

Brazil Rock

● Anchorages and Harbors visited and points of interest

of Me and my Boats

TABLE OF CONTENTS   Page

1
THE EARLY YEARS

My love for boats began in Nova Scotia. I was born in Middle LaHave, a farming and fishing community on the banks of the LaHave River. The river is navigable for approximately 10 miles from LaHave to the town of Bridgewater. At Middle LaHave it is about ¾ mile wide. When I was five years old my family moved to Watertown, Massachusetts, where I grew up. But we spent a lot of time every summer "down home" in Nova Scotia.

During the era of schooner fishing on the Grand Banks there were many shipyards on the LaHave River building fishing schooners. In 1901 there were 1,141 men working on 61 fishing schooners sailing out of the LaHave River. As a young man my father served on a fishing schooner for one trip to the Grand Banks. He told me he was seasick for the first two weeks and when he got home he informed his father he would never go back. Instead he became a carpenter and restricted his boating to the LaHave River.

Before they were married my mother and father lived on opposite sides of the river, my father in Middle LaHave and my mother in Pentz. There was a lot of travelling back and forth in boats, since the nearest crossing was in Bridgewater. My father had a small motorboat, the *Mystery,* and Saturday evenings they would motor up the river to the movies in Bridgewater. Dad knew every part of the river by heart and they would return in the dark of night with no lights.

Looking Across the LaHave River
from Pentz to Middle LaHave

During our summer visits to Nova Scotia as boys, my brother and I spent many hours in boats on the river. My family had a small wooden rowboat that we sanded and painted each year, and that was the source of most of our boating. This rowboat and the small dories around the area had thole pins to hold the oars in place when rowing. Thole pins are the forerunners of oarlocks. They are hardwood pins set in the gunwales in pairs to hold the oars in place when rowing. A second means of propulsion was sculling, which was accomplished by placing an oar in a cutout at the top of the transom and moving it thwartwise with a turning motion

Our other "boat" was a raft that we built using logs we towed home from around the banks of the river using the rowboat. We put the wheelhouse from the *Mystery* on our raft for a place to change into our swimming trunks. The wheelhouse was the only remaining part of the *Mystery.*

In addition to the rowboat and the raft we occasionally were allowed to use a small double-ended motor boat owned by our Uncle Gabe. It was powered by a single cylinder Acadia engine made in Bridgewater. The engine had a very large dome-shaped appearance with an exposed heavy flywheel. Closing a knife switch and cranking with a retracting handle on the flywheel started the engine. If the knife switch was opened to turn off the engine, and then closed again at just the right time, the engine would run backwards and the boat would go in reverse. There is an Acadia engine in the Maritime Museum in Greenwich, England.

The Acadia Engine

I don't remember doing much with toy boats in Nova Scotia. I guess we were too busy with bigger boats, and with swimming and fishing in the river. But it was different in Watertown, Massachusetts. King Street, where we lived, was on a fairly steep hill. The street was not paved. At the top of the hill, at right angles to King Street, was Grandview Avenue, also unpaved. Unlike King Street, Grandview Avenue was level, and following rainstorms it was the site of many large mud puddles. The mud puddles were great places to sail small boats.

My brother and I and the neighborhood kids made little pine boats, which we raced in the mud puddles. We designed them with shallow draft especially for mud puddle sailing. They were spoon-shaped with a single square paper sail and a fixed rudder at the "handle" end to keep them going in a straight line. We made many other small boats of soft pine during the early years at King Street, but none of them were as unique as the mud-puddle boats.

Mud-Puddle Sailboat

My next experience with boats was at the Watertown High School Model Yacht Club. Mr. Black, the machine shop teacher, founded the club. We made model yachts about three feet long from plans and materials provided by Mr. Black. There was a balsawood vane on the stern to control the rudder and keep the boat on a steady course in relation to the wind. When they were finished we raced the boats in a lagoon on the Charles River in Boston. A race consisted of several trips running down the lagoon with a following wind and then tacking back against the wind. Members of the club were stationed along the lagoon to tack the boats when they approached the sides. My boat, the *Falcon*, won the trophy. My brother's boat, the *Dolphin*, had won the trophy several years before We never raced against each other because our boats were different sizes.

Falcon – My Trophy-Winning Model Yacht

In my senior year at Watertown High School I thought it was time to have a bigger boat – one that I could sail in. I had seen plans for an International Moth in an issue of Popular Mechanics, and planned to build one in the basement of our house on King Street. My father was a carpenter, so all the necessary tools were available. The Moth was scow-shaped with a length of 11 feet and a beam of 4 feet. I made the frames from oak flooring fastened with brass screws. Plywood would have been the ideal sheathing material, but it was not available at that time so the hull was sheathed with ½" clear pine. The mast was hollow and was laminated of fir flooring. A major problem was finding enough clamps to clamp the 18' mast together while the glue dried, but this was solved by borrowing clamps from some of the neighbors. Another problem was that the plans called for a pivoting centerboard made of 1/8" steel, which I had no way to fabricate. A friend of my dad worked in a machine shop and was kind enough to make the centerboard for me.

The Popular Mechanics article included patterns for the single sail. It recommended making a full size pattern of newspapers taped together, and then using this pattern to cut the cloth for the sail. I did this on the living room floor and then sewed the sail on my mother's treadle sewing machine.

When the boat began to take shape my mother got quite upset and said, "I don't know why he has to build a boat. When he gets it finished, if he ever does, he won't be able to get it out of the basement". My dad said, "If he finishes it I'll get it out". When the boat was finished he was true to his word – but it wasn't easy. He had to cut some of the floor joists and move them in order to get enough clearance between the basement stairs and the floor framing above to get the boat out through the basement door.

For a mooring we filled a small nail keg with concrete and imbedded a 3/8" eye bolt in the top. We hoisted the boat onto pads on the roof of my father's 1935 Dodge and drove it to a cove in the Charles River about a mile east of Watertown Square. There we put in our mooring. We had one minor setback – during the launch I stepped on a broken bottle in the water and got a nasty cut on the bottom of my foot requiring a trip to the family doctor after the launch and a quick sail. At the time we put in my mooring there were only a few boats moored in the cove. No permit was required. Now the cove is the site of the Watertown Yacht Club and it is crowded with large powerboats.

Other boating experiences during high school years were as a member of the Watertown Sea Scouts. The Sea Scouts had a 50' power boat, the *Viking*, given to them by the Coast Guard. We went on weekend cruises to several different ports, and many weekends we went fishing in Boston Harbor. The *Viking* had chronic engine problems and frequently had to be towed back in by the Coast Guard. My father was on the committee and went on some of the fishing trips. On one of the trips, when the sea was rough and the Viking was rolling from side to side, many of the crew were seasick. After having been seasick for two weeks on a fishing schooner, dad apparently got over it for good; he was down in the galley steaming some of the clams that had been brought along for bait – and eating them.

Sailing the Moth on the Charles River

After the Moth and the Sea Scouts there was a long boat hiatus; after high school I was drafted and spent three years in the army, went to MIT, and married my next door neighbor, Joyce Skinner. Joyce and I moved a lot – we lived in Watertown, Massachusetts; Boston; Waltham; Burlington, Vermont; and Watertown, New York. During this time my brother had the Moth. He lived in Natick, Massachusetts on Lake Cochituate and had two sons and a daughter. They all sailed the Moth on the lake. They maintained it and made a new mast when the original one delaminated. Eventually, however, the Moth deteriorated to a point where it no longer could be repaired and had to be broken up

2
THE POCKET CRUISER

In 1964 Joyce and I were living in Lexington, Massachusetts. Our family had grown – we had two small boys. Following my family tradition we went to Nova Scotia for our vacation many summers. During one of our visits I was reading a copy of the National Fisherman and came across a review of a book named "Pocket Cruisers" by J. D. Slightholme. It was a book about small British cruising boats that were easily trailed behind a family car. I was intrigued by the idea of having a small cruising sailboat that could be kept in the driveway and towed to a launching ramp for weekend cruising. Shortly after returning home I bought a copy of the book. It contained drawings and photographs of many "pocket cruisers" ranging in size from 17-1/2' to 22'. In addition it had information about navigating and sailing these small boats, living small, road trailing, and useful tips about a variety of related subjects. Many of the boats had twin keels, so they would sit upright when grounded by a falling tide. This was a useful feature for boats sailed on the English Channel side of England, where the tide is 25' and the moorings dry out at low tide.

A few weeks after I bought the book there was an ad in the Boston Globe by Bay Village Boats. The ad included a picture of an Alacrity, one of the boats in the J. D. Slightholme book. I called Bay Village Boats and made arrangements to visit them, review their brochure, and discuss the boat with them. Bay Village Boats consisted of Clinton Wells and his wife; they operated out of their apartment in Boston. They told me about the good experiences they had sailing the boat, including seeing whales on a cruise from Boston to Provincetown. I agreed to meet Clinton the following Saturday in Marblehead, where they had one of the boats. Joyce and I and our son John, then 8 years old, sailed the boat in Marblehead Harbor and I placed an order for a boat and trailer. Incidentally, from this humble beginning Bay Village Boats became Wells Yachts and grew to be the largest sailboat dealer in New England.

The layout of the Alacrity's cabin was pretty simple. There were port and starboard quarter berths plus a single berth on the port side at the bow. Between the port quarter berth and the forward berth was a low compartment containing the head. Forward of the starboard quarter berth was a sink, and forward of this was a full-height locker with shelves. In order to make sleeping space for the two kids I filled in a triangular space by the forward berth, making it into a double berth with one short side, large enough for Tim who was only 3 years old.

Our water was carried in heavy plastic folding containers, which could be hooked up to a manual galley pump. We had a small two-burner alcohol stove that we set up on the compartment containing the head, and we could store food for a weekend in a portable cooler and in the locker forward of the sink. Auxiliary power for the boat was a small British Seagull outboard motor. A lightweight Danforth anchor was held in chocks on the foredeck.

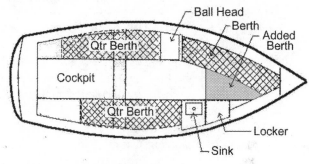

Alacrity Layout

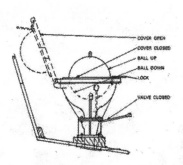

The Ball Head

The head was a "Ball Head". The bowl of this unusual head was covered by a half rubber ball with a handle on top. To use the head a valve to the ocean is opened, the ball is pushed down and pulled up filling the bowl with water, then the valve is closed and the cover is hinged back out of the way. After the head has been used the cover is hinged back down, the valve is opened, and the ball is pushed down discharging the contents straight out into the ocean. The Ball head was designed and manufactured at a time when there was little concern about pollution and "no discharge" regulations had not yet been enacted.

The Alacrity had twin keels made of oak and ballasted with lead. The draft was 1'-10", so it could be sailed in very shallow waters. Navigation equipment was rudimentary; we had a compass to determine direction, a lead line to measure water depth, and nautical charts for the areas where we sailed.

Since we now had a small cruising boat we would need a dinghy to get ashore when we anchored, so I designed and built one. It had to be lightweight so I could carry it, stable when stepped into, and easy to tow. I designed it with a double-V shaped bottom for stability and easy towing, and built it over the winter.

I had one other project over the winter to prepare for sailing the new boat the next summer. I took the Basic Boating course given by the Charles River Power Squadron at Lexington High School. The Charles River Power Squadron was the local branch of the United States Power Squadrons (USPS). Organized in 1914, USPS is a non-profit educational organization dedicated to making boating safer and more enjoyable by teaching classes in seamanship, navigation and related subjects. Although I was quite familiar with boats and boating, I thought it would be a good idea to take some formal courses, since I would be sailing in coastal waters. After passing the Basic Boating Course I joined the squadron and continued my boating education for a number of years, eventually taking all the courses the Power Squadron had to offer, including celestial navigation. In order to be a useful first mate, Joyce also took the Basic Boating course, joined the squadron, and then proceeded to take additional courses up to Advanced Piloting.

Alacrity at Westport   Alacrity Crew Members John & Tim

Everything was ready in the spring of 1965. The dinghy was finished, the Alacrity had been modified to accommodate the two kids, and we had an anchor, a compass, a lead line, life jackets, charts, and all the other necessary gear.

That summer we took a one-week vacation in Westport Massachusetts. The cottage we rented was on the Westport River, so we took the Alacrity along with us. One day John and I sailed out to the Buzzards Bay entrance tower to get a close look at it. The tower is located about 8 miles from the mouth of the Westport River. It was the first manned lighthouse in the United States built over open water (i.e., lacking a foundation on dry land). It was built in Texas on the model of an offshore oil platform and floated to the site. It was then sunk in place and its four steel pilings driven down to the bedrock and filled with concrete. The tower has accommodations for five men, and a flat roof for helicopter operations.

Buzzards Bay Entrance Tower

We motored out of the river and then put up the main and genoa, since the wind was light from the southwest. At about half way to the tower the wind picked up and I decided to change from the genoa to the working jib. John, who was eight years old at the time, took the tiller and I went forward to change the sail. He did a great job steering and I changed the sail with no difficulty and we sailed out around the tower. When we got back to the entrance to the river the tide was low and the current coming out of the river was so strong that we were slowed almost to a standstill. It took like what seemed forever to finally get by the narrow entrance, with the outboard running at full throttle.

Our first overnight cruise was from Westport to Cuttyhunk, the western-most of the Elizabeth Islands separating Buzzards Bay from Vineyard Sound. We had a nice sail to Cuttyhunk in light winds, and because of the shallow draft of the Alacrity we had no difficulty finding a place to anchor in shallow water at the perimeter of the moored boats in Cuttyhunk Pond. We all were very excited to navigate to our destination, anchor, prepare our meals, and spend our first night on the boat.

There were many other weekend cruises. We joined a Charles River Power Squadron rendezvous at the Castleneck River, which is southwest of Crane beach at the north end of the Annisquam River. To get there we launched the Alacrity in the Annisquam River near the Gloucester High School and motored up the river to the rendezvous. The launch was easy but the retrieval was a different story. There was a lot of traffic on the river and the waves from passing powerboats kept floating the boat off the trailer before we could haul it out. After getting the boat settled on the trailer many times and having it float off, there finally was a long enough period of time between passing boats to complete the retrieval. Fortunately I had previously modified the trailer by adding a bow post and winch. Before this change retrieval was extremely difficult, even in ideal conditions.

One interesting cruise was to the Parker River to the west of Plum Island. For this trip we launched the boat at Essex, Massachusetts, and motored up the Essex River to Ipswich Bay and then on to the Parker River. The ramp at Essex was crowded with small outboard motorboats and we had to wait our turn, but we didn't have the problem of passing powerboat traffic that we had in the Annisquam River. We anchored near the mouth of the Parker River in three or four feet of water at high tide. The water was very clear, and as the tide went down we watched crabs scurrying around on the sandy bottom. As the tide fell we bounced gently on the bottom, and at low tide we were hard aground with the boat sitting upright on the twin keels. We could have stepped overboard and walked ashore.

The Crowded Launching Ramp at Essex

I made another filler for the forward bunk to convert it to a double for two adults, and invited my sister Verne and her husband Bob to go with us on an overnight cruise from Falmouth to Edgartown. The ramp at Falmouth turned out to be unusable and I had to pay to have the boat hoisted in and out of the water by a small crane. We had a nice sail to Edgartown and were lucky enough to get a mooring in Edgartown harbor. The Alacrity was by far the smallest boat in the harbor and it was interesting to sit in the cockpit eating dinner at the cockpit table I had made, surrounded by all the large yachts. We sailed south to Katama Bay, which is quite shallow, and even with our 1'-10" draft we ran aground. For some unknown reason

Bob, who was a real landlubber, immediately jumped into the dinghy, lost the oarlocks overboard, and almost fell in. He didn't realize that with such a shallow draft he easily could have gone overboard and pushed the boat to deeper water, which we did shortly after.

I had several other adventures, or misadventures, with the Alacrity. I planned to launch the boat in Essex and sail up the Essex River and to the Isles of Shoals with my brother Bert and his son Parker. This was to be a trial run for a trip we planned to make to the All-Star family conference on Star Island at the Isles of Shoals later that summer. When we were almost to Essex I realized that we didn't have the boom. I had to unhitch the trailer, leave it and the boat by the side of the road, and drive back to Lexington to get the boom.

Two other misadventures were in Gosport Harbor at the Isles of Shoals when we were there at the family conference. After we arrived at Gosport Harbor I anchored the boat in the harbor not far from the hotel and we rowed ashore. The water was fairly deep and the bottom was kelp – not very good holding ground for our Danforth anchor. When I looked out the hotel window the next morning there was no Alacrity to be seen. I searched the harbor with my binoculars and finally spotted it near the shore on the other side. I got dressed and rowed across the harbor, where I found the Alacrity tied to a fisherman's mooring. There was white paint on the rudder. The boat apparently had dragged into the fisherman's white boat, which kept it from running onto the rocks, and when he left in the morning he tied it to his mooring.

Several days later I took one of our friends out for a sail. The weather turned nasty and we hastened back to the harbor, only to be blown onto submerged ledges near the shore. Because of the shallow draft I was able to jump overboard and push the boat to deeper water with no difficulty.

In the fall of 1965 we bought a "junk" lot on Baskin Road in Lexington. The lot dropped off sharply from the street and had been used as the neighborhood dump. It was cluttered with old tires, signs, and piles of leaves dumped there by the neighbors. John and I cleaned it up, rented a U-haul trailer, and took everything to the town dump. One day while we were cleaning up the lot a pile of leaves came tumbling down on us. There was a boy at the top of the slope shaking a tarp. I said, "Don't dump leaves down here". He said, "We always dump our leaves here". I told him not to do it anymore, that I owned the lot and would be building a house on it.

After the cleanup we surveyed the lot with a hand level, a steel tape, and a pole marked in inches and feet. When the survey was done I proceeded to design a house to fit the difficult lot. It had two levels at the front and three levels at the back. The front entrance was between the upper and middle floors and was from a bridge at street level. Living, dining, and kitchen were on the middle level. On the downhill side away from the road were large windows and glazed doors opening from the living room onto a secluded balcony. Construction started in late fall and it took about a year to build. We sold the Alacrity before the house was finished – we were running out of money and there wouldn't be time for sailing anyway because I planned to do much of the interior finish work and landscaping myself. As a result we were boatless for a number of years after moving into the new house.

The Baskin Road House under Construction

3
SNOOPY

By the winter of 1970-71 we were ready to buy another boat. Our financial situation had improved and the new house was in pretty good shape; most of the interior finish and landscaping was done. We began seriously looking at ads for used boats in the Boston Globe. (This was long before the Internet.) In April we bought a used Catalina 22 and trailer. The accommodations of the Catalina were much better than the Alacrity. It was not as solidly built as the Alacrity, but we thought it would be OK for the type of sailing we would be doing. There was a double V-berth forward, with a marine head under a removable panel. The head could be made private by means of a sliding curtain. On the port side was a dining arrangement that could be converted to a double berth, On the starboard side there was a single berth and an impractical sliding galley. After buying the boat I immediately designed and built a permanent galley at the forward end of the berth, and converted the berth to a quarter berth. This was the only change I made.

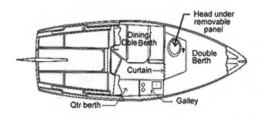

Catalina 22 Layout   Joyce – New Galley to Right

The Catalina had a cast-iron swing-keel that could be retracted for trailing behind the car and sailing in shallow waters. The draft was 5'-0" with the keel down and 1'-8" with it retracted. Power was a British Seagull outboard, the same as the one on the Alacrity. Speed under power was four knots. This is useful information when navigating by dead reckoning in poor visibility. Like the Alacrity, the Catalina had a compass, a lead line, and nautical charts. It also had a Danforth anchor in chocks on the foredeck. New navigation equipment was a hand-bearing compass.

The Alacrity never had a name, but we let the boys name the Catalina. They named it "*Snoopy*".

We found a good launching ramp in Buzzards Bay at Mattapoisett and frequently launched *Snoopy* there and sailed in Buzzards Bay. We had an unusual experience on our first weeklong cruise. The first leg was to

Hadley Harbor, which is across Buzzards Bay and just west of Woods Hole. There was a dance on the pier next to the launching ramp in Mattapoisett when we arrived Friday evening, and we were unable to launch the boat until the dance was over at 10:30 PM. The sail across Buzzards Bay in a light southwest wind was uneventful, but as we approached our destination I became a little nervous. We had never been to Hadley Harbor before. There is a lighted bell buoy off the entrance to Woods Hole and Hadley Harbor, which we easily found, but the entrance to the harbor is not easy; it is rather narrow and has several sharp turns. There was no moon, the night was pitch black, and we had no searchlight. As we motored in from the bell, a boat shining a searchlight came out of Woods Hole heading for Hadley Harbor. We were close enough that we were able fall in behind and follow it into the harbor. When the boat had anchored we pulled up next to it to thank them for guiding us in. To our surprise the boat was the *Scrimshaw*, owned and sailed by Dick and Jackie Stone, our next-door neighbors in Lexington.

The next day we motored through Woods Hole and sailed west to Tarpaulin Cove on Naushon Island. There were several other boats anchored in the cove. In the early nineteenth century there were as many as 2,000 sheep on Naushon Island, and Tarpaulin Cove was a busy place where farmers did business with crews of incoming vessels. A privately-maintained lighthouse was built on the west side of the cove in 1759 and was replaced by the federal government with a new tower and caretaker's

The Lighthouse at Tarpaulin Cove

house. Naushon Island is now owned by the Forbes family and the only buildings at Tarpaulin Cove are a farmhouse and the lighthouse tower. The keeper's house was demolished, probably in the 1930's when the Coast Guard automated most of the lighthouses.

We left Tarpaulin Cove in the afternoon heading for Oak Bluffs on Martha's Vineyard. There was very little wind and we motored most of the way, arriving at 7:00 PM. In the morning there was spaghetti floating around in the harbor. The noisy people on a small powerboat near us had spaghetti for dinner the previous evening. The skipper obviously had too much to drink and threw up his share of spaghetti into the harbor. We rented bikes and toured the island in the morning. It was very hot in the afternoon so we went for a swim to cool off. We left Oak Bluffs in the late afternoon and sailed to Edgartown, arriving and picking up a mooring in time for dinner The next morning we rowed to Chappaquidic and walked to the Dike Bridge, where Ted Kennedy drove off the Bridge, and his passenger, Mary Jo Kopechne, was drowned. After seeing the small bridge and the narrow curving road we thought driving off the bridge would be an easy mistake to make on a dark night.

There was heavy rain and wind during the night and we had to fend off swinging boats. The weather was still nasty in the morning. About noon we went ashore and picked up supplies in Edgartown, returned to the boat, and left Edgartown at 2:30 PM. The wind was strong at first, but then dropped to three knots. We went through Woods Hole and anchored in Hadley Harbor at 8:15 PM. The next day we left Hadley's in mid-morning. and arrived at the Mattapoisett ramp in the early afternoon. I forgot to pull in the dinghy painter when we got to Mattapoisett and it fouled on the propeller and was cut into 3 pieces. I also forgot to take the rudder off when hauling the boat, and scraped the rudder on the ramp. Fortunately it was not badly damaged. All in all it was a good cruise anyway.

Boat Shed at Hadley Harbor

4

DISCOVERING THE MAINE COAST

John and I went on a weekend Maine cruise in July of 1972. We drove to South Portland in our Chevy Nova, hauling *Snoopy* on the trailer, with the dinghy on a roof rack and the outboard motor in the trunk. We parked at the launching ramp and since it was late in the day we slept on the boat and planned to launch in the morning. In the morning we took the dinghy off the roof and went to take the outboard out of the trunk – the trunk was locked and we didn't have the key. I managed to get the trunk open by smashing the lock using a screw driver and hammer from *Snoopy's* toolbox.

Dinghy on Car, *Snoopy* on Trailer

After launching *Snoopy* we sailed to Jewel Island and anchored in the cove on the northwest side of the island, now known as cocktail cove (see chart on page 174). We went ashore and walked across the island to the Punch Bowl (picture on page 61), an interesting round pond created by the shore and offshore reefs. We ate berries from the many berry bushes along the path. We then hiked towards the southwest end of the island, where we explored concrete lookout towers, underground tunnels and bunkers, and gun-emplacements constructed during World War II when there was a lot of concern about German submarines along the coast. There also was a large house used for officers quarters, barracks for enlisted men, and other one story buildings, all in various stages of deterioration. The buildings are now gone, but the concrete constructions still remain. On the way back we were caught in a heavy shower and got soaked.

The next morning we were socked in with fog. It lifted about noon but closed in again after a short time. There was a 35' ketch with no one aboard that had been anchored near the shore ever since we had arrived. At each low tide it grounded and heeled over. A fisherman told us that the owner had been called back to Boston and had to leave it anchored in the cove. In the afternoon at low tide it heeled over and began to fill with water. When the tide rose the boat righted itself, but it was full of water. Later in the afternoon the Coast Guard arrived, pumped it out, and towed it to Cliff Island, where fisherman could watch it until the owner returned.

World War II Concrete Fortifications on Jewel Island

At 5:10 PM the fog was still dense and there was no wind, but we left anyway to go to Falmouth Foreside for the night. We motored out of the cove and turned southwest between Jewel and Cliff Islands. We motored at a speed of four knots from buoy to buoy, around the end of Cliff Island, through Chandler Cove, and then on to Falmouth Foreside behind Clapboard Island. We set courses between the buoys and then determined the amount of time that should be required for each leg of the trip. In that way we would know when we should be at or near the next buoy and could circle around to find it if it didn't appear when expected. Fortunately our navigation was good and we didn't miss any buoys. We arrived at Falmouth Foreside amid a crowd of moored boats, went in to the dock and got a mooring from Handy Boat. The fog was so dense that we had trouble maneuvering between the moored boats and finding the dock. We hadn't seen a thing since leaving Jewel Island except for the buoys, a dim view of the end of Long Island after passing through Chandler Cove, and the moored boats at Falmouth Foreside.

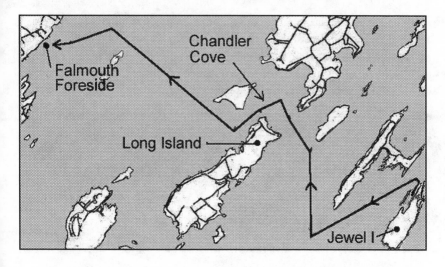

From Jewel Island to Falmouth Foreside in Thick Fog

This was our first experience navigating in Maine fog, an experience that would be repeated many times in the next 30 years. After going to the mooring we rowed ashore to relax and have dinner at "The Galley", a restaurant at Handy Boat. I was thankful for the navigation knowledge I had acquired from my Power Squadron classes.

The following morning it was still foggy, but not "pea soup" like the day before. There also was a light breeze. We left the mooring at 09:18 and were able to sail all the way to South Portland on the starboard tack. The keel hit part of a wreck on the way, but there was no damage. At one point a huge freighter loomed out of the fog and crossed very close on our bow, looking like a great cliff. We arrived at the ramp at 11:45, hauled the boat, and headed for home. A great trip and one to remember.

We all made one other weekend trip to Casco Bay that year. We anchored in a cove at Great Diamond Island and stayed overnight. While we were there John went for a short sail in the dinghy, which I had rigged with a temporary plastic sail. The following day we sailed to Mackerel Cove at Bailey Island, tied up at a float, and had dinner at a restaurant near the top of the ramp from the float.

By August of 1973 it was time for a real Maine cruise. Bill Watters, a boat owner and colleague of mine at Bolt Beranek and Newman, told me about some of his favorite anchorages in Maine and I was anxious to experience them first hand. Joyce, John, Tim, and I drove to Rockland, Maine on a Saturday and launched *Snoopy* at a ramp right next to "Captain Pete's" restaurant at about 5:30 PM. The ramp was dirty and in unattractive surroundings, but it was an easy launch with no other boats there. We headed for Pulpit Harbor on North Haven Island with a Northwest wind of

15 knots, just about perfect for the course we were on. The entrance to the harbor is marked by Pulpit Rock. The Cruising Guide to the New England Coast, which was our cruising bible for many years, said that Pulpit Rock was difficult to find, and gave explicit instructions for finding it. The book was right; we thought we had missed it, but just before dark we spotted it at last. We entered the harbor with Pulpit Rock to starboard and then tacked to starboard and anchored in Minister's Cove, where we spent a quiet, peaceful night.

In the morning we discovered that we hadn't stocked the galley very well. There was no milk or juice for breakfast. Also, John had planned on donuts, so he was disappointed because they also were among the missing.

Pulpit Rock

The Cruising Guide said that ospreys had been nesting on top of Pulpit Rock for many years, so John and Tim took the dinghy and rowed to Pulpit Rock to get a closer look at the ospreys. They were instructed not to land so they wouldn't disturb the birds.

The next stop was to be Stonington, where we could buy the supplies we needed to properly stock the galley. Wind was light southeast. We left Pulpit Harbor Sunday morning and sailed northeast along North Haven Island on the starboard tack, then tacked down East Penobscot Bay to Deer Island Thorofare and Stonington. At Stonington we bought supplies, including Marie McHenan's delicious homemade donuts. With this accomplished we motored to McGlathery Island, highly recommended by Bill Watters. There are two good anchorages at McGlathery Island: one on the west side between Round and McGlathery Islands, and one in a cove at the northeast side of the island (see chart on page 192). We went to the cove and found only one other boat there, the *Clarion* from Marion. We had previously seen the *Clarion* in Hadley Harbor! The weather was just about perfect – sunshine, blue skies, and blue water. John had a new two-man tent that he had won in a bike race. We found a nice clearing in the woods, just out of sight of the harbor on soft mossy ground under the spruce trees.

The Beach at McGlathery Island   Tim Rowing Joyce Ashore

John and Tim pitched the tent there and stayed ashore for the time we were at McGlathery. They also cooked some of their meals on John's small one-burner camp stove. We had a pair of walkie-talkies and we used them to communicate between *Snoopy* and the shore crew. Tim was a good rower and he ferried supplies between the boat and the camp and rowed us back and forth.

The day after we arrived, the *Clarion* from Marion left and another boat named the *Quissetta*, from Quissett (another Buzzards Bay harbor) arrived. Bob and Judy Gray had sailed the *Quissetta* from New Brunswick and were on their way back to Quissett. They told us about their favorite clamming spot between McGlathery and the small unnamed island to the east, which was connected to McGlathery at low tide. We did no clamming during this visit, but I did dig for clams with success during later visits to McGlathery Island.

The Campsite at McGlathery Island   Joyce Writing in the Log

We stayed at McGlathery for two days, exploring the rocky shoreline, the neighboring small island, and just relaxing and enjoying the good weather and the beautiful surroundings. On Tuesday morning we left McGlathery Island with a reefed main and reefed jib. The weather was still sunny and clear, but the wind was 20 knots, gusting to 25 knots. The boat was well balanced under reduced sail and sailed along nicely. We arrived at Mackerel Cove, Swan's Island shortly after noon and anchored near the ferry dock. The ferry moves cars and people between Swan's Island, Bass Harbor, and Mt. Desert Island. We rowed ashore and were lucky enough to get a ride to the town of Atlantic, about a mile down the road. The town consisted of a store/post office, a church, and several houses. At the store we bought a few supplies and some post cards, which we mailed at the post office in the same building. The man who was the postmaster also ran the store. He was a small man with a bald head and a limited number of teeth. After walking back to the harbor we watched the ferry load up four cars and about 30 people. We followed the ferry out of the harbor and headed for Bass Harbor.

Bear Island Light at the Entrance to Northeast Harbor

We looked in at Bass Harbor and decided to go on to Northeast Harbor, which would have more possibilities for shore activities in case of a change to inclement weather. At Northeast Harbor Joyce prepared us a great dinner of ham, potatoes, peas, salad, and dessert.

Wednesday morning the weather was still sunny and beautiful. The boat on the mooring next to us was the *Spice* from Mattapoisett, the third boat from a Buzzards Bay harbor we had seen. John, Tim, and I went ashore for water, ice, and a few more supplies, including steak from the Pine Tree Market. We tacked out of Northeast Harbor a little after noon in a southwest wind of 15 knots and sailed to Buckle Harbor, at the northwest corner of Swan's Island. This is a nice little secluded harbor. A great blue heron was wading around in shallow water at the perimeter of the harbor, but there also were lots of mosquitoes and little flies around the boat. John and I went ashore looking for a place to pitch the tent, but there were no appropriate campsites. The land surrounding the harbor was heavily wooded, dark, and covered with thick damp moss. We cooked an excellent steak dinner on a portable charcoal grille in the cockpit, and with the help of "Off" we also ate in the cockpit, the weather remaining perfect.

The Public Dock at Northeast Harbor

In the morning the sky was overcast and there was a barely perceptible breeze. After a pancake breakfast John and Tim rowed around the harbor and tried fishing, but had no luck. We put up the sails and sailed out of the harbor, ghosting along. Our destination was Duck Harbor at Isle au Haut. The wind was variable, light to non-existent. About a half mile from Duck Harbor John leaped into the dinghy and began rowing like a mad man for the harbor. He beat us in, even though we had started the motor. There were no other boats. This was fortunate, since the Cruising Guide said the harbor was large enough for only two boats. Shortly after we arrived another boat, the *Dragonfly III,* from Falmouth came in.

Tim and John went ashore and found a good campsite. They also found a tide pool loaded with sand dollars and large snails. John pitched the tent and they slept ashore for the night. They made cocoa for breakfast on John's camp stove and kept in touch with us via the walkie-talkies.

The next morning the sky was overcast, the weather was warm, and the visibility was limited to less than a mile. We hiked to the top of Duck Harbor Mountain on a well-marked trail and were rewarded with a great view of the harbor. We then hiked to Western Head, where there was a good view out over Isle au Haut Bay. Tim, who had lost much of his sight due to a brain tumor when he was only five, did amazingly well on this hike over rough ground. When we got back to the harbor there was another boat there, the *Maya* from Harpswell. They ate lunch in the harbor and then motored out.

Tent at Duck Harbor

On top of Duck Harbor Mountain

Our plan was to sail from Duck Harbor to the Fox Islands Thorofare and find a place to stay overnight, then go on to Rockland the next day. We left Duck Harbor in the late afternoon. It was a hazy day with very little wind and we drifted along on a course to Fox Islands Thorofare. About half way across Isle au Haut Bay we noticed fog moving in from the south. I was able to get a fix from two sights, one at Saddleback Ledge Light to the south, and one at Smith Island to the west, then the fog closed in. We couldn't see anything. The wind died so we took down the sails and turned on the outboard and headed for bell "4" at the entrance to Fox Islands Thorofare (see chart on page 25). We were motoring along at four knots when suddenly the engine stopped. I was able to start it a few minutes later and discovered that the cooling water was not circulating; the engine was overheating again and stopped running. The Seagull engine has no shroud; the block is completely exposed. It occurred to me that pouring cold water over the outside of the block might provide sufficient cooling, and hopefully it would keep running. I restarted the engine and John and I took turns steering and pouring water over the block with the teakettle. It worked fine, and the engine kept running.

Based on the fix I had obtained and our speed of four knots under power I established the time it would take to reach the bell at the entrance to the Fox Islands Thorofare. When my calculations indicated that we should be close enough to hear the bell we turned off the engine and listened. We heard it, turned on the engine and motored to the bell. Channel Rock with its beacon, although close by, was barely visible to starboard through the thick fog. We then changed our course and headed for can "5", where we planned to turn in to Carver Cove on a compass course of 140 degrees.

Crossing Isle au Haut Bay   Saddleback Ledge Light*

When the calculated time had elapsed there was no can to be seen. Carver Cove is fairly large and I was sure we were close to the can, so we turned to 140 degrees and headed in to Carver Cove (we hoped). John was steering. I told him to hold the course and I would go up on the bow with the leadline, take soundings, and let him know when to turn off the engine. At first it was too deep for the leadline, which was only 30' long, but soon it reached bottom and the depth gradually decreased. At a depth of 16' I notified John, he shut off the engine and I lowered the anchor. With the engine off we could hear a dog barking to starboard and a halyard slapping to port. We must be in Carver Cove!

We had supper and turned in for the night. About 4:00 AM we were awakened by a spectacular thunderstorm. The lightning lit up the boat with a brilliant white light. There was heavy rain, thunder, and lightning for about an hour before it finally ended and we went back to sleep. When we awoke in the morning the sun was shining brightly and the water was dead calm. We were indeed in the middle of Carver Cove! What a satisfying experience. Once again I thanked the Power Squadron for the navigation knowledge I had acquired.

We left Carver Cove at 10:50 AM and motored to North Haven, where there was a good grocery store. We bought milk, juice, cellar-cooled beer,

*Originally there was a keeper's house attached to the Saddleback Ledge lighthouse tower. One evening during a storm the keeper was sitting at his kitchen table when a duck crashed through the window and landed fluttering at his feet. Later another duck crashed through the plate glass in the lantern room, broke the lens, and put out the light. This bombardment continued from early evening until midnight. In the morning the keeper picked up 124 dead ducks at the base of the tower. The keeper's house was demolished when the light was automated by the Coast Guard in the 1930's.

5

ANEMONE

After our weeklong Maine cruise we began to get serious about cruising and thought it would be nice to have a boat that was not so crowded with a crew of four. We looked at a lot of boats at the February boat show in Boston and were impressed by the layout of the Midship 25. It had a center cockpit and an aft cabin, which would be ideal for the two boys. We ordered a Midship 25 from the dealer at the boat show, but there turned out to be some problem at the factory and they later informed us that they couldn't get a boat for us for the coming summer. They did, however, locate a used Midship 25 in Connecticut that we could purchase. The list of equipment and the price were satisfactory, so we went ahead with the purchase. In June of 1974 John, Tim, and I drove to Connecticut in our Oldsmobile Delta 88 to pickup our new boat and trailer. It was a long drive, so when we got there we slept overnight on the boat and then drove back to Lexington the next day. The boat was too heavy for the rear springs on the car, so the back end of the car was down a lot, but it drove alright anyway. One of the first things I did after getting the boat home was to replace the rear shocks on the car with air shocks, which could be pumped up at the neighborhood gas station to level the car.

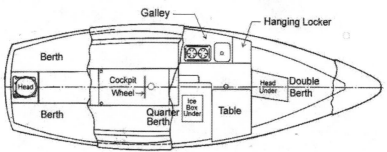

Midship Layout

The layout of the Midship is unusual. The main cabin is forward. It has a double V-berth with a marine head under a removable panel. On the port side are a galley and a small hanging locker. There is standing headroom at the galley. On the starboard side are a dining table and a large quarter berth. Seating for the table is on the V-berth and the end of the quarter berth. There is a large ice box under the forward end of the quarter berth. It is a good icebox but a real nuisance; as soon as we all would get seated for a meal something would be needed from the icebox and the person sitting there would have to get up, remove the cushion, open the icebox cover, and take out whatever was needed.

Aft of the forward cabin is a large center cockpit with a wheel. Aft of that is another cabin with two berths, a marine head, and a small icebox. The main and aft cabins have hinged hatches at the companionways rather than the usual sliding type hatches (see pictures on pages 37 and 51).

Our Midship was powered by a seven horsepower inboard gasoline engine, had a large cast iron swing keel, and a retractable rudder that could be partly raised for sailing in shallow waters. Again we had a Danforth anchor in chocks on the foredeck.

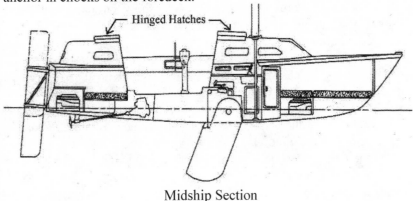

— Hinged Hatches —

Midship Section

We named the new boat *Anemone* (windflower) and I painted the name and a windflower on the transom.

Our first three boats, including *Anemone*, had marine heads that discharged directly overboard. When they were built this was perfectly legal. Since then, no-discharge laws have been enacted and are in effect in most harbors and bays. Cruising boats now must have heads that discharge into separate holding tanks, or heads that have built-in holding tanks. Many Harbors now have free pumpout stations.

I made additions and improvements to all our boats, either to make them sail better or to make them more comfortable. The Midship was no exception. I made a teak grating for the cockpit and and added a plywood enclosure for the head in the aft cabin, complete with a small sink that drained into the head.

Our first trip on *Anemone* in June 1974 was fraught with difficulties. We drove to Mattapoisett and found the ramp crowded with boats of every size and description. Colvin Marine, from whom we bought the boat, had failed to provide the bow wheel that was required to use the trailer extension. During the time we were waiting to use the ramp the tide went down and we needed the extension. John and I searched around and found an old wheel by a trash container and were able to attach it to the trailer. After waiting for five hours we finally were able to launch *Anemone*. We headed for Hadley Harbor and about half way there the fog set in. John steered and I navigated. The wind was light and we were motoring. At the appropriate time we turned off the motor and heard the bell near the entrance to Woods Hole and Hadley Harbor. As we headed in from the bell the fog lifted enough so we were able to see the can and nun at the entrance to the harbor, and we motored in and anchored.

After spending the night in Hadley Harbor we sailed back to Mattapoisett and landed *Anemone* at the float. I went ashore to get the trailer and was dismayed to find that it was nowhere to be found! I called the police department to report the missing trailer and was told they had towed it off because it had no numberplate on it and therefore wasn't registered. I had taken off the trailer light and put it in the trunk of the car before launching; the numberplate was attached to the light and therefore was not on the trailer. I paid a $15 fine and got the trailer back. Retrieval of *Anemone* went very smoothly. The side rails on the trailer centered the boat and simplified the process so it was easier to retrieve than *Snoopy* had been.

Anemone on Mattapoisett Ramp

In July we launched *Anemone* at the ramp in Essex to sail to the Isles of Shoals, where we were going to attend the All Star II conference on Star Island. We motored up the Essex River, which is very shallow. On *Anemone* we had added a depth sounder and a hand-held wind meter to our navigation equipment. At one point the depth sounder told us we were going to run aground, and we did! Not a problem. We cranked up the keel and were on our way. We anchored and stayed overnight in Essex Bay, which is not well-protected from Ipswich Bay and the Atlantic Ocean. The boat rocked incessantly, keeping us awake for most of the night. In the morning we left and sailed to the Isles of Shoals with an east wind of eight knots. Our stay at Star Island was uneventful, but on the trip back we wallowed around in winds from two to five knots, alternatively motoring and sailing. We had no genoa jib and made slow progress. Shortly after this trip I located a used mainsail with a longer foot and made an oak extension for the boom to accommodate it. This addition and a new genoa jib, greatly improved *Anemone's* light-wind performance.

Raising *Anemone's* Mast   Retrieving *Anemone* at Marion

Anemone was easy to rig. The mast was raised by first installing the boom and then using a winch to haul on a line attached to the end of the boom. This is illustrated in the left photograph above.

After launching *Anemone* at Mattapoisett a few times we discovered a good ramp in Marion, which was a much nicer port than Mattapoisett, and we made Marion our home port for the rest of our sailing days. We soon thought it would be convenient to have a mooring in Marion so we wouldn't have to trail, launch, and retrieve *Anemone* every time we went for a weekend sail. Bill Coulson, who ran Barden's Boat Yard, was the harbormaster, and although he said a mooring was available he gave us a hard time and moved us around from place to place. A friend of ours, Don Sullivan, came to the rescue. He had just inherited a mooring from a friend of his who had moved back to Mexico. Don rented the mooring to me for the price he and Dick Stone were paying for a mooring that was closer to the dock. (Don and Dick were co-owners of the *Scrimshaw*, a Tartan 27.)

With *Anemone* on a mooring we would only haul her occasionally for long trips, including to the Isles of Shoals for the All Star II conferences, Boston Harbor for the Tall Ships parade, and Maine in August.

We had several uneventful weekend sails before hauling Anemone on the Marion Ramp to go to Maine. On one of the weekends the wind was 20 to 25 knots and we were pleased with the way Anemone handled the wind and waves, although there was some pounding because of the hull shape.

6

TO MAINE ON *ANEMONE*

For our first Maine cruise on *Anemone* we once again drove to the ramp at Captain Pete's in Rockland. Hauling *Anemone* up and down the steep hills and narrow curving roads in Maine was a little hair-raising at first. The trailer had surge brakes, which were activated when the car brakes were used, and this helped a lot. The Oldsmobile Delta 88 had plenty of power so there was no problem getting up the hills. At one point we were stopped by the Maine State Police. They measured the width of the trailer with a tape to see if it was within the legal limit of 8'-0". It just passed and we were free to continue on our way.

Captain Pete's Restaurant was under new management and was renamed "The Black Pearl". According to the Chamber of Commerce there had been $25,000 worth of improvements, but it still looked a slum from the ramp side (see photo on page 26). We chanced to meet Jack Chesley and his wife on the dock. Jack was a member of the architectural firm Morehouse Chesley and Thomas, with whom I had worked as an acoustical consultant. He said we should sail to Carvers Harbor where Dick Morehouse had a summerhouse and was going to show a movie he had made of "Old Coot". Old Coot had lived in an old yellow school bus for years and Dick had designed a house for him. Jack gave us directions for walking to Dick's house from Carvers harbor.

We sailed to Carvers Harbor, anchored for the night, and went ashore to see the movie. Dick was quite surprised when we appeared, and welcomed us to the small group assembled for the movie showing. Along with the movie we were treated to drinks and refreshments. After the movie we returned to the boat. During the night the anchor dragged and we drifted onto some rocks. I got up about 5:30 in the morning, raised the keel, and re-anchored in a deeper spot. A retractable keel certainly has its advantages.

That morning we raised the anchor, sailed east from the harbor, crossed Isle au Haut Bay, passed Merchant Island on Merchant Row, and went between Wreck and Round Islands to McGlathery Island. Once we were anchored in the cove the boys rowed ashore and pitched the tent in the same place as the previous year. We spent two beautiful days at McGlathery apparently not doing anything, since I found nothing about the two days in the log even though there is a picture of Joyce writing in it.

The weather was beautiful at McGlathery Island and only a few boats came and went. That changed in time, and many places that were secluded and visited by only a few boats now and then, became crowded anchorages overrun with boats. At McGlathery "No Camping" signs were erected.

Two Beautiful Days at McGlathery Island, August, 1974

After a delightful stay at McGlathery Island the boys struck the tent and we headed for Northeast Harbor for re-provisioning. The wind was light and we alternated between motoring and sailing with the main and genoa. Our course took us across Jericho Bay, through York Narrows and Casco Passage, across Blue Hill Bay and Bass Harbor Bar, and then up Western Way to Northeast Harbor. York Narrows is a well-buoyed narrow and crooked passage between small islands and reefs at the northeast corner of Swans Island. We went in to the float at Northeast Harbor and then took the boat out to a mooring we had gotten from the harbormaster. We then rowed in and went to the Pine Tree Market. Thanks to the Pine Tree Market, that evening we had a delicious dinner of steak, fried potatoes, and tossed salad, with Sara Lee banana cake for dessert.

When we turned in for the night there was an empty mooring off our bow. The next morning there was a black fishing boat, the *Midnight* on the mooring. We assumed that it had arrived at midnight. For breakfast there were more goodies from the Pine Tree Market. We had Jones sausages, fried eggs, and cinnamon-nut rolls. After breakfast we went ashore and

Anemone at Northeast Harbor   The *Midnight*

took showers at the Yachtsman's building, left our laundry at "The Shirt Off Your Back", and went to the Pine Tree Market for more supplies. Then it was lobster rolls for lunch at "Flick's", followed by ice cream cones at the drug store.

The next stop was to be Somes Harbor at the head of Somes Sound. Before heading up Somes Sound we stopped at the Mobil dock for water and ice. The water tank was under one of the berths and there was no deck-fill. The hose had to taken into the cabin; water ended up everywhere and had to be mopped up. Not a good detail!

When we left Northeast Harbor there wasn't much wind, but when we entered Somes Sound all Hell broke loose; the wind was blowing in all directions and the current was against us. We eventually got to Somes Harbor and picked up a guest mooring. At Somes Harbor we learned how to keep others from using your mooring; one of the moorings had a sign on it that read, "Rotten Chain. Use at your own risk". In the sound the hills are quite high and slope steeply down to the water on both sides, much like I've seen in pictures of Norway fiords, but around the harbor the hills are much lower and it is not as secluded as we expected.

In the early morning we motored down the sound with a favorable tide. We wanted to get to the narrows at the entrance before the current turned against us. Tim steered happily down the middle of the sound, with warnings to change course occasionally to avoid lobster pot buoys. There had not been many times he could steer because of his limited eyesight. Our eventual destination was Port Clyde, where we had made arrangements to meet our neighbors, Dick and Jackie Stone, who were sailing the *Scrimshaw*. Fog set in off Southwest Harbor and we motored to Bass Harbor Bar from buoy to buoy. At Bass Harbor Bar the buoys had been changed from those indicated on the charts, and we motored around a buoy in a state of confusion wondering where we were. Finally the fog lifted slightly and Bass Harbor Bar lighthouse appeared to starboard. We followed the shore into Bass Harbor where we filled the gas tank, bought ice, and ate a lunch of tunafish sandwiches, potato chips, cookies, and milk.

From Bass Harbor we set sail in a light SSW breeze to cross Blue Hill Bay. The wind died and the fog returned so we motored from buoy to buoy again, through Casco Passage and York Narrows, across Jericho Bay, and to a secluded anchorage between Devil and Bold Islands called "Hells Half Acre". This is in an archipelago between Deer Island and Isle au Haut, consisting of exposed granite ledges and many small islands covered with spruce trees and granite outcroppings. It includes McGlathery Island and is one of the most beautiful areas on the Maine coast. To the north are Deer Island Thorofare and Stonington, and to the northwest is pretty little Mark Island Light (picture on page 81).

Hells Half Acre

In the morning we had orange juice, French toast, coffee and cocoa for breakfast. The fog was dense. John and Tim put on foul-weather gear, took a walkie-talkie and compass, and rowed around exploring Hells Half Acre. In the afternoon there was a spectacular thunderstorm with a lot of rain, lightning, and wind, followed by an equally spectacular rainbow. After the storm Joyce had a double scotch and I had a martini on the rocks, thankful that the mast had not been hit by lightning. Next was a typical Boston Saturday night dinner of baked beans, grilled hot dogs, salad, white and pumpkin bread, and sugar cookies for desert.

We had canopies on all our boats but the alacrity. They were useful as sunshades in harbor, and could be rigged as tents during rainy weather, as shown in the picture above. Canopies rigged as sunshades on *Anemone* and *Pearl III* are illustrated on pages 32 and 162.

We were awake the next morning at six and underway at seven. We went east of Spruce, No Mans, and Gooseberry Islands to a cove on the southwest side of Merchant Island, where we anchored and had breakfast. At 9:00 we headed southwest across East Penobscot Bay on our way to Carvers Harbor. There was a favorable 10-knot breeze so we bypassed Carvers Harbor and continued on to Tenants Harbor. Halfway across West

Penobscot Bay the wind died and we motored the rest of the way to Tenants Harbor.

Southern Island Light   Cod End and The Big White House

We passed Southern Island light at the entrance to Tenants Harbor and tied up at the Cod End dock in the harbor at 6:00 PM. Joyce, Tim, and John walked up the hill to the grocery store and bought bread, milk, donuts, eggs, margarine, and lemon coffee rolls. Joyce said the store was a dusty, dirty mess, and that the outside and parking area also were a trashy mess. While they were at the store I bought ice and fresh haddock at Cod End. Mrs. Miller, the proprietress, brought a complete haddock out from a wood-lined walk-in cooler, flopped it down on the counter, and proceeded to filet it. We had it for dinner and it was excellent. With the haddock we had fried potatoes, carrots and peas, and milk and tea. While we were ashore we were told that the big old white house next to Cod End was being remodeled and would be turned into an inn with a restaurant.

There was a beautiful sunset that evening. As a matter of fact there was a beautiful sunset at Tenants Harbor almost every time we went there. We didn't know if it was a coincidence or if the frequency of beautiful sunsets had something to do with the topography to the west.

We turned in at 9:00 PM. At 3:30 AM I woke up because the boat was moving strangely. The fathometer showed 14' of water but we weren't swinging properly. When I pulled on the anchor rode a lobster pot buoy popped up, and once I untangled the pot warp from our anchor rode everything was back to normal. We got up at seven and had a leisurely breakfast of orange juice, scrambled eggs, donuts coffee and cocoa. We sailed out at 10:30 with John at the helm and Tim reminiscing about last night's good fish. We arrived at Port Clyde at 1:05 PM for our rendezvous with the Stones. Joyce went shopping once more at the general store, which was clean and well stocked and quite a contrast to the one at Tenants Harbor. I tried to get the battery charged at the store, but their charger was not very good and we had to leave the battery overnight.

The *Scrimshaw* arrived at five with the Stones, Dick, Jackie, and son Jimmy aboard; also Ace, their black Lab. They went shopping at the store and then we left our moorings intending to motor up behind Hooper Island, where Dick said there was good anchorage. The Scrimshaw was in the lead with Dick, John, Tim, and Jimmy aboard, and they hit some rocks and went aground. John was the lookout on the bow. He saw floating seaweed just before they hit the rocks, but not the rocks, which were hidden by the seaweed. The *Scrimshaw* was stuck on a falling tide and there was no chance of getting her off until high tide the following morning. *Scrimshaw* did not have a retractable keel like *Anemone*. We moved *Anemone* back and anchored in 20' of water. Jackie slept on *Anemone* because the *Scrimshaw* was heeled over so badly.

Scrimshaw Aground

In the morning the tide was not quite as high as the night before. A small powerboat came along and tried to pull the *Scrimshaw* off the rocks but wasn't able to do it. With our instructions he finally got her off by pulling on the main halyard from the top of the mast and sliding her off sideways. We motored over to the dock and picked up *Anemone's* battery, which was finally charged, and then headed northeast past Tenants Harbor and up Muscle Ridge Channel to a small cove near Owls Head lighthouse. We stopped there long enough to have lunch, then put up the main and genoa and headed for Camden up West Penobscot Bay. The wind was behind us at 20 to 25 knots and John had a busy time steering. In Camden Harbor we tied up at the public float and asked the harbormaster about moorings. He told us we could raft up at a float out in the harbor for the night. We Went ashore searching for a shower with no luck; everything was closed so we

Anemone and Scrimshaw Sailing up West Penobscot Bay

sponged ourselves off and went out to dinner. We ate at a nearby fish and chips type place that turned out to have good food, although the atmosphere left something to be desired. Then we had ice cream cones and walked around town. We went in to the bookstore near the harbor. It had a downstairs devoted to nautical books of all kinds – the most complete collection any of us had ever seen. There also were easy chairs so you

Raftup at Camden

could browse in complete comfort. A delightful place. In the morning Jackie went to the Laundromat and Joyce continued her search for showers, which she finally found at the Lock Marina. The slips in the Lock Marina were several feet above the harbor and were accessed by a small lock that raised and lowered the boats.

After taking a shower Joyce and Tim went to the bakery for pie and do-nuts, and to the market for meat. In the early afternoon we left Camden and headed for Pulpit Harbor. John and Jimmy sailed the *Scrimshaw* and Dick and Jackie came with us on the *Anemone*. Once again we had difficulty finding Pulpit Rock, but as before it finally showed up.

Our joint cruise ended in Pulpit Harbor. From there the Stone's continued their cruise and we sailed to Rockland, where we hauled the boat and headed for home. This time we didn't have any trouble at the ramp. It was relatively clean and there were no clam boats to delay our retrieval. Another great Maine cruise, but it would be the last one with our whole family. John was almost 20 and had other interests, and Tim was prone to seasickness and would only be going with us on special occasions.

Getting Ready to Haul at Rockland   Ready to Roll at Rockland

7

TALL SHIPS AND MAINE ON *ANEMONE*

During 1975 we didn't get to Maine and there were no extended cruises. Joyce was attending summer school for much of the summer and I was very busy at the office. Our sailing was confined to weekends and there were no log entries for the entire year.

In the spring of 1976 I had Burr Brothers in Marion lift *Anemone* off the trailer with a crane so John and I could paint the bottom. Burr Brothers also scraped barnacles from the keel well and swabbed bottom paint up inside. They then lifted the boat into the water and John and I headed for the mooring. The motor quit and we unrolled the roller-furling genoa and sailed to the mooring. Barden's had not yet replaced the winter stake with a mooring float so we had a terrible time getting moored. By the time we were ready to leave for home it was dark and it took us two hours to get the trailer light to work. Then to top things off the light and number plate fell off somewhere on the way home.

There were several weekend cruises in Buzzards Bay early in the summer and in July we sailed to Boston to see the Tall Ships Parade on the 10th. Tim and I went to Marion the morning of the 8th, hauled *Anemone* at high tide and drove to Scituate, where we launched her. There was a nice concrete ramp in Scituate and the launch went well. Joyce and John drove to Scituate in my MG Midget and met us the next day. Joyce was not thrilled with John's driving; she said he drove too fast, tailgated, and made quick lane changes.

The rule for boats watching the Tall Ships Parade was to be anchored by 8:00 AM, so we decided to sail to Hingham Harbor and get an early start from there in order to be anchored in time. Before going to Hingham Harbor we sailed out where we hoped to see some of the ships sailing to Boston from New York. We saw only one – it was motoring. We then headed for Hingham Harbor. By the time we had passed Nantasket Beach and turned west it was dark and the weather had deteriorated. A thunderstorm brewed and rain bucketed down so hard I had trouble seeing the chart through its plastic cover. John was at the helm and I was giving him steering instructions. There were lights everywhere: white lights, red lights, green lights; flashing lights, quick-flashing lights, and occulting lights. I was totally confused. Then I remembered advice I had read in Pocket Cruisers. J.D.Slightholme wrote, "Faced with a mass of lights one need only pick out those which assist. The rest, unless they lie athwart the course, can be left alone". I followed his advise and picked out the needed lights, gave John instructions, and we got safely to Hingham Harbor where we anchored, ate supper, and went to bed.

We got up at 5:30 in order to get to the anchorage in time. Anyone moving in the harbor after eight was to be fined $50,000! As we were about to anchor, the spark plug fouled and the fan belt came off, but we got anchored anyway. We were having a lot of trouble with the Midship engine.

It was a beautiful sunny day with just enough wind to fill the sails of the tall ships, and the parade was fabulous. It was led by a fireboat shooting multiple sprays of water into the air, followed by the Constitution* firing a cannon every minute. Then came the tall ships from all over the world with their sails set. The crowd of boats observing the parade was equally

The Tall Ships Parade

*The *Constitution* is the oldest commissioned naval vessel afloat in the world. She was launched in Boston, Massachusetts in 1797 and was given her name by president George Washington. One of her first duties was to defeat the Barbary pirates in the First Barbary War. During the war of 1812 against Great Britain she defeated five British warships, including HMS *Guerriere,* which earned her the nickname "Old Ironsides"

fabulous, with horns blowing, bells ringing, and spectators climbing their masts to get better views and photographs of the ships.

We had hot dogs on toasted rolls for lunch. When the parade was over we maneuvered away from the crowded boats, sailed back to Scituate, and hauled *Anemone*. Joyce and I drove home to Lexington trailing the boat, with John and Tim following us in the Midget. John's driving was greatly improved over the trip from Lexington. He kept back a reasonable distance and didn't make any foolish maneuvers. All in all it was a very satisfying and exciting trip!

In August Joyce and I drove Anemone to Maine. We arrived in Rockland at dead low tide and found the ramp and surroundings overflowing with trash and garbage. Disgusting! We walked to the ferry dock and asked if there were any other launching ramps around. The ramp at Rockport was highly recommended, so we drove there. The ramp was clean and neat and there was a nice parking lot. There was a fee of $1 to use the ramp, and $1 a day for parking. We had a dinner of fresh fish and blueberry pie at "The Helm" on route 1. After returning to the ramp we launched *Anemone*, tied up at the public float, and went to bed for the night.

Parking Lot at Rockport

In the morning we sailed across West Penobscot Bay, through Fox Islands Thorofare, across East Penobscot Bay and on to McGlathery Island, where we anchored in the northeast cove. The weather was nice and we were happy to be back at McGlathery Island again. There were two other boats in the cove, but we were able to anchor in our favorite spot, have a grilled steak for dinner, and turn in. In the morning we walked across the sand bar to the small-unnamed island, climbed the hill, and picked and ate raspberries. When we returned the tide was rising and we had to wade across the bar. We just loafed around on the boat for the rest of the day

The next day after a leisurely breakfast and a walk we set sail for Marshall Island to the east, which was highly recommended by Don McGinley in "Cruising Penobscot Bay". He said Sand Cove on the east side of the island was the prettiest sand beach anywhere on the coast. Unfortunately the wind was east and the weather turned chilly and overcast, so we looked in at the west side of the island. There was nothing there but rock cliffs with waves dashing against them. We went around to the east side and there were two fishing boats that had the whole cove sealed off with fish nets. It might have been nice in good weather with a west wind and no fish nets, but what we saw was a very nasty looking place. Goodbye Sand Cove!

After our aborted visit to Sand Cove we went to Burnt Coat Harbor on Swans Island. There were large swells, little wind, and it was chilly and overcast. We motored most of the way and anchored well up in the harbor near the lobster wharf. We walked up the hill and mailed some post cards, but didn't stay ashore long because the sky was dark and a thunderstorm was predicted. Later I rowed ashore and bought two 1-1/2 pound lobsters for dinner. The place were we were anchored was somewhat exposed. We could see the light on Hockamock Head and could hear the surf crashing outside on the rocks. Also, there was a lot of kelp and poor holding-ground, so we moved behind Harbor Island where there was better protection and good holding-ground. A shouting man greeted us at Harbor Island. His name was John Putnam and he invites anyone who goes near the island to come ashore to visit with him and his wife and hike the trails.

Hiking with the Putnams on Harbor Island

There was thunder and lightning most of the night and in the morning it was foggy and damp. John Putnam invited us to their farmhouse and to walk the surrounding trails. We had tea and coffee and then went for a vigorous hike around the island in the fog, wearing our foul weather gear. After the hike we had drinks aboard their boat, *Western Bell*, which was a wooden Controversy built locally. We then went back to *Anemone* and had dinner. More thunder and lightning!

We later learned that John Putnam's home was in Acton, Massachusetts and he was very active in town affairs. He had been town moderator for 10 years and had founded several organizations that were involved in improving the life of individuals and communities.

In the morning the fog finally lifted and the sun came out. We motored out the narrow passage between Swans and Harbor Islands, then to the east of Black Island and Great Gott Island and on to Northeast Harbor.

The Three-masted Schooner *Victory Chimes** at Northeast Harbor

We stayed overnight at Northeast Harbor, and in the morning mailed postcards and got money at the bank. After a lunch of lobster and crabmeat sandwiches at Flick's we went back to the boat and went out Eastern Way Out of curiosity we poked into Seal Harbor, which is a vacation area for

*Three-masted schooners (known as Tern Schooners) were developed in the late 19th century for coastal trading. They required smaller crews and were less expensive to operate than square-rigged vessels. They also could sail closer to the wind. The *Victory Chimes* was built in 1900 and is the last remaining tern schooner on the east coast.

the Fords and Rockefellers. We didn't see any of them and decided they were all at the Republican National Convention. From there we crossed Frenchman Bay and went in to Inner Winter Harbor, which is a beautiful little harbor. It was full of lobster boats of all colors; red, yellow, purple, blue, etc. We picked up an empty mooring that a lobsterman pointed us to, rowed ashore, and walked up the hill to Chase's Restaurant. Joyce had a lobster dinner and I had a fisherman's platter. Chase's was recommended to us by a man on a Cape Dory 25 who had come in to the harbor and moored next to us. It was a good recommendation.

Inner Winter Harbor

In the morning the weather was beautiful – a bright sunny day with a brilliant blue sky and cumulus clouds. We headed west and went through Casco Passage intending to go through Eggemoggin Reach, but the wind turned out to be unfavorable. We turned southward, crossed Jericho Bay, and went to Hells Half Acre behind Devil Island, the same place we were fog-bound in 1974. There was a large blue sloop anchored near us and a Silhouette came in from the west. The Silhouette is a 17-1/2 foot British pocket cruiser that was in Slightholme's book. We were surprised that there were two adults and a 12-year-old boy aboard this tiny boat! Then I remembered that we had sailed on the 18-1/2' Alacrity with two adults and two children, and once with four adults!

The sandpipers were peeping and other birds were singing. We had hot tomato soup and crackers, then switched to a martini for me and a Scotch and water for Joyce. Dinner next! It doesn't get any better than this!

The next morning we motored over to Stonington, looked around the Atlantic Hardware store, then went to the market next door and bought orange juice, cereal, block ice and cubes, cheese, and Marie McHenan's donuts. From Stonington we motored over to the cove between McGlathery Island and Round Island. We anchored, made sandwiches, and took lunch and beer ashore for a picnic. After returning to the boat we headed for Isle au Haut. We planned to anchor at Point Lookout, but it was crowded with eight boats, so we went to Burnt Island Thorofare. The anchorage is a tricky place to get to. We followed the Cruising Guide instructions carefully to avoid a big rock in the passage, then we dropped the hook when "just west of a line between the wharf on Burnt Island and the wharf on Isle au Haut". Very tricky! After anchoring we ate dinner and went to bed.

We had orange juice, boiled eggs, and donuts for breakfast, and then left, expecting to see the big rock exposed at half tide. It didn't show up but we did see it under the water, a big ugly looking light-colored ledge just below the surface. We motored through Isle au Haut Thorofare and came to Seal Trap, a narrow inlet surrounded by ledges. It was well named – there were about a dozen seals sunning on the rocks and swimming outside. The Cruising Guide recommended trying it on a rising tide in a shoal-draft boat, but we could sail in such shallow water that I cranked up the keel to go in and we tried it on a falling tide. It looked like a puddle surround by seaweed – hardly worth the effort. We motored out and headed for Duck Harbor.

There was a large float in the center of Duck Harbor with a green dinghy tied up to it and a sign saying, "Do not tie up here". At about noon the *Miss Lizzie*, a large powerboat from Isle au Haut, pulled up to the float and disgorged eighteen people with cameras and other paraphernalia. They were rowed ashore in the green dory in three trips, were landed where we had landed our dinghy on the previous trip, and hiked into the woods, probably heading for Duck Harbor Mountain. I had mixed feelings about all this – on one hand it was nice that all these people could get to see this beautiful island, but on the other hand their presence destroyed the tranquility, one of the main reasons for going there.

Shortly after the *Miss Lizzie* arrived The *Skimmer*, a light-blue Tartan 34 from Concord, sailed in and anchored. The captain was an obnoxious type who shouted orders to the crew to let us know that he was doing the best he could with the bunch of idiots he was stuck with. His boat swung around and would have hit us if I hadn't told their "idiot" kid to grab our bow pulpit and push us off. I then offered to move our boat farther up into the harbor, to which captain Skimmer noted, "It shoals up pretty fast in there", letting us know how knowledgeable he was. Not a word of thanks. I guess he didn't realize that we could anchor *Anemone* in less than two feet of water.

A dory anchored near the *Skimmer* was about to swing into it, so Mrs. Skimmer hopped into their dinghy to fend it off. This prompted the captain to shout, "What are you doing off the boat?" Joyce said, "I hope she's jumping ship!"

Old Campsite at Duck Harbor

View from Western Head

After *Miss Lizzie's* passengers disappeared we rowed ashore and walked out to Western Head. We were saddened to see John and Tim's old campsite with two picnic tables where the tent had been and a Johnny-on-the-Spot and a trash container nearby.

We ended up the sailing season in Marion Harbor on October 11th with an end of the season stew that was a mixture of many items: chunky sirloin burger, Dinty Moore's beef stew, and canned vegetables. It was a beautiful day so we took a short sail out around Bird Island. After returning to the harbor we had sandwiches and beer, then rowed ashore and drove home. I returned the next weekend to haul the boat and drive it home for the winter.

Anemone at Home

8

FARTHER EAST ON *ANEMONE*

John and I launched *Anemone* in June 1977 at the Marion Ramp. It was a messy day with a nasty northeaster. We motored down to the town dock, but couldn't put up the mast because of the wind. We were told by a fellow at the dock that it was gusting to 80 mph in Chatham. We had a supper of macaroni and cheese with tuna and turned in for the night at the dock.

We rigged the mast and lifelines in the morning and then went to the Sippican Lunch for a breakfast of eggs, bacon, fried potatoes and coffee, plus a donut for John. After breakfast we motored to the mooring, rowed ashore, and drove home.

After a few weekend cruises in Buzzards Bay we hauled *Anemone* in late July and Joyce and I headed for Maine. Our plan was to go farther east than we had been before. We launched *Anemone* at Rockport. The weather was overcast and somewhat windy, but we sailed across West Penobscot Bay, through Fox Islands thorofare, across East Penobscot Bay, and on to McGlathery Island. In the morning it was raining and blowing 25 to 30 knots. We started out to motor to Stonington, but with the rain, wind, and poor visibility all the little islands looked the same. We had difficulty navigating so went back to McGlathery and ate a lunch of hamburgers with fried potatoes, green peppers, and green beans. If we had planned ahead and plotted a course before we left we probably would have made it to Stonington.

It was beautiful and sunny the next day so we motored to Stonington and bought Marie McHenan's delicious donuts, red wine, ice, and stove alcohol. Then we put up the main and working jib and headed east through Deer Island Thorofare and on to Northeast Harbor. The harbormaster said there were no moorings available, but his assistant said there were two out by a blue lobster boat, numbers 46M and 46L. When we got to the blue lobster boat there were two empty moorings, but the numbers were different from what we were told. We picked up number 7652, went ashore, and bought a homemade apple pie and homemade oatmeal bread, (both by Mrs. Pervear), a Boston Globe, and a few other items.

The next day we went out Eastern Way and past Schoodic Island. The wind was west to southwest. The Cruising Guide to the New England Coast says "To be headed east by Schoodic whistle before a summer sou'wester with Mt. Desert fading astern and the lonely spike of Petit Manan Light just visible on the port bow is about as close to perfection as a man can expect to come on this imperfect earth." We were pleased to be heading east. The Cruising Guide also says that Petit Manan Bar can be

Petit Manan Light* – the Bar is out of the Picture to the Left

dangerous. The tide runs strong and the sea is always rough and confused. Another problem is frequent fog. However, when we crossed the bar the current was slack and the weather was clear, bright, and sunny! We passed easily between the buoys marking the passage across the bar. After crossing the bar we turned northward to a cove at Trafton Island (see chart on page 144). There was one other boat in the cove, a wooden Crocker type named *Tante Loj* from Essex, Connecticut. The skipper looked very disappointed to see us appear at his secluded anchorage and nobody on the boat gave us a "rec". For dinner we had a steak from home, along with fried potatoes, tossed salad, and Mrs. Pervear's homemade apple pie.

Sailing *Anemone*   The Bridge at Moosabec Reach

*The original lighthouse tower at Petit Manan was poorly constructed and was weakened by storms. It swayed badly in gale winds and keepers working there felt as though the top would be blown off. In one storm the huge weights from the clockworks in the tower broke loose, smashing 18 steps of the cast iron staircase on its way down to the base of the tower. In the late 1800's radical repairs strengthened the tower and stopped the swaying.

We turned in early and got up early to head east again. After going through Moosabec Reach we stopped at Jonesport (see chart on page 145). There was no room at the floats so we picked up a nearby mooring and rowed ashore, where we mailed postcards and bought lobsters for dinner. We also bought two bags of ice cubes, two ten pound blocks of ice, bread, donuts, margarine, and batteries for the radio. It was low tide and the ramp leading to the dock was very steep. Joyce said it was nearly vertical, which was an exaggeration, but although unhappy about it she managed it both ways. After lugging all the stuff back to the boat in boat bags we left Jonesport, crossed Chandler Bay and anchored in Bunker Cove between Great Spruce and Little Spruce Islands at 5:00 PM. There was a Pearson 43 named *Deirdre II* from New York there when we arrived.

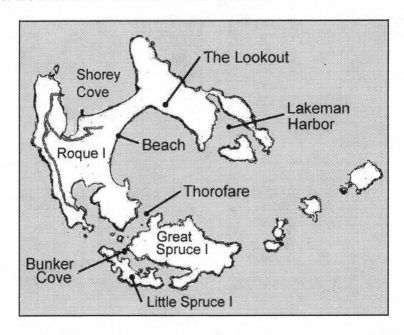

Roque Island

We cooled a bottle of white wine hung on a string over the side, cooked our lobsters, ate dinner, and washed the dishes. After dinner the captain of *Deirdre II* invited us over for a chat. Aboard were Hugh and Mable McTeague and their 16-year-old daughter, who had Down syndrome. The *Deirdre* was quite a floating motel – hanging plants in the main salon, pictures on the bulkheads, a bowl of ripe peaches on the table, and the stereo playing the "Sorcerer's apprentice". They bought such a big boat because they planned to live on it in a couple of years. They had looked at a Hinckley but it didn't have accommodations comparable to the Pearson.

The next morning we motored through Roque Island Thorofare to Roque Island Harbor. We anchored near the beach (which is the main feature at Roque Island) and rowed ashore. It was a gorgeous sunny day with a fresh southwest breeze, and the beach was spectacular – like a south sea island beach. We walked to the north end of the beach and climbed to the rock outcropping at the top, where there is a spectacular view of the beach. The rock out-cropping at the top was covered with the names and initials of previous visitors. We thought this defacing of the location was somewhat gauche and declined to add anything.

The Beach* at Roque Island

After returning to the beach we were greeted by a young woman, Betsy Rich, who had driven a jeep to the edge of the dunes. She said she lived on the island in the summer and told us a little about its history. It was owned, and had been for almost 200 years, by two families, the Gardners and the Monks. At one time the Gardners sold their property to a man named Shorey, but bought it back after a short time. The houses are on the northwest side of the island at Shorey Cove. She also told us that 75 boats from the Cruising Club of America were expected in the area in a day or two. Following our discussion with Betsy we motored back to Bunker Cove and re-anchored.

I climbed the adjacent cliff and took pictures of *Anemone* from above while Joyce watched marine life and different colors appear on the side of the cliff as the tide ebbed. The rise and fall of the tide at this location is 16 feet. When I returned to the boat we had steaming clam chowder, grilled ham and cheese sandwiches and beer for lunch. After lunch we read, napped, and watched large sailboats come in and anchor in the outer cove.

*In his book "Ready About" G. Peabody Gardner, whose great-great grandfather acquired Roque Island in 1805, said that according to legend the Indian name for the beach meant "The Racecourse". According to the legend a race was run down the beach and back by two Indian braves with the prize to be the hand of the chief's daughter in marriage. One brave fell dead from exhaustion at the ¾ mark and the other fell dead at the finish line

Two boats that didn't favor the cliff side of the cove were aground when the tide went down. There was a lot of activity around us; people going clamming up in the cove, and a man in a small outboard zooming in and out. We assumed that he was a warden checking for clamming licenses.

Anemone at Bunker Cove

The last evening we were there a sailboat named *Irish Mist*, that had been anchored farther up in the cove in a deep spot, came out and anchored not far from us. In the morning they were hard aground and heeled over all the way. When the tidal range is 16 feet one must choose an anchoring location with great care! I checked the chart and decided they should have stayed where they were originally.

Irish Mist Aground at Bunker Cove

After two days we left Bunker Cove motoring in the fog and headed for Moosabec Reach. There was a lot of seaweed in the reach that wrapped itself around the propeller and slowed our progress. We found the bridge in the fog, but after passing under it we were unable to find the nun near the end of the reach (see chart on page 145). We motored in a square with no luck so we anchored and ate breakfast. After breakfast the fog lifted and we could see the tiny little nun. I hooked the seaweed off the propeller with the boat hook and we were under way again.

The current and the visibility, although limited, allowed us to cross Petit Manan Bar without difficulty, but by the time we got to Frenchman Bay the fog socked in again. The wind was 15 knots on the beam and we were moving at a good speed, blowing our horn twice each minute. When the can ran out of Freon the spare can was defective and wouldn't blow. As a makeshift Joyce got a large frying pan from the galley and proceeded to bang on it with the ladle. We heard another boat blowing, indicating it was on the opposite tack, but its horn became less and less loud. Finally there was a scale-up and we were approaching Eastern Way as expected.

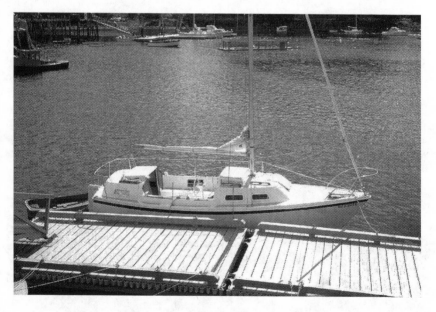

Anemone at the Rockport Public Float

The remainder of the trip back to Rockport was uneventful. We tied up at the public float, backed the trailer down the ramp, and hauled the boat with no difficulty. This turned out to be our last Maine cruise on Anemone.

9
PEARL II

After our 1977 Maine cruise on Anemone we were thinking about a cruise to Nova Scotia sometime in the near future. Although a Midship 25 had made a trans-Atlantic voyage we were not comfortable with the idea of taking ours offshore and felt we should have a heavier, fixed-keel boat. Graves Yacht Yards in Marblehead was a Cape Dory dealer and was advertising in the Boston Globe. The Cape Dory 30 was a ketch and Graves had one in their show room. I had always been partial to split rigs and had even toyed with the idea of converting Anemone into a yawl by adding a small mizzen, but gave it up because of structural difficulties. So we went to Graves Yacht Yards and looked over the one they had in their showroom. I expressed an interest in buying it. They gave us a price that I thought was reasonable and I placed an order. We ordered cockpit cushions for comfort and a genoa jib for light weather sailing. We took possession in November 1977 with the understanding that our boat would be moved to a location in one of their sheds where I could work on it during the winter, since I had several additions and improvements I wanted to make.

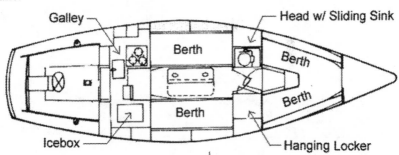

Cape Dory 30 Layout

Designed by the legendary naval architect Carl Alberg the Cape Dory 30 has a mostly traditional layout. The main cabin has port and starboard settee berths with a removable folding table in between. Aft of the berths is a galley with a gimbaled alcohol stove on the port side and a large icebox on the starboard side. The top of the icebox is at a perfect height to use as a large, stand-up chart table. Between the stove and icebox is a counter with a deep sink, resulting in an open U-shaped galley. In the bow there is a cabin with two single berths that can be converted to a double. The main and forward cabins are separated by a small enclosed area with a head and sliding sink on the port side, and a hanging locker on the starboard side.

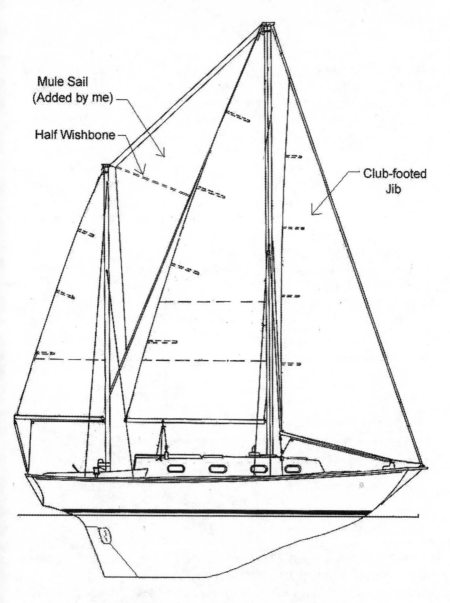

Mule Sail (Added by me)

Half Wishbone

Club-footed Jib

The Cape Dory 30 Sail Plan and Underbody

The normal sail plan of the Cape Dory 30 includes a club-footed jib, making the vessel self-tacking. This is advantageous when entering and leaving harbors. Sheeting the mizzen in tight and releasing the sheets on the other sails facilitates anchoring or picking up a mooring. When this is done a ketch backs down in a straight line; the bow doesn't fall off the wind like the bow of a sloop does. These two features are helpful in coastal cruising where many harbors are visited and there is frequent anchoring and mooring. Add to this the advantage of heavy weather sailing in a boat that is well balance under reduced sail – jib and mizzen. Because of these advantages I disagree with many sailors who say that a 30 footer is too small for a ketch rig. The ketch rig may not be as efficient as a sloop rig, but for coastal cruising it can't be beat.

The Cape Dory 30 is a full keel yacht. This underbody configuration is ideal for cruising in Maine, where lobster pot buoys and warps are a frequent hazard. The pot warps slide harmlessly along the keel, and when under power they are rarely sucked into the propeller in its protective aperture.

Pearl II's cockpit has a teak steerer box with a helmsman's seat and a traditional spoked teak wheel. There is seating on cushions, port and starboard, on a bridge deck, and on both sides of the steerer box.

Pearl II's Cockpit and Wheel

The anchor, as on our other boats, was a Danforth held in chocks on the foredeck.

During the winter I drove to Marblehead most weekends to work on the boat. I measured the cockpit and laid out a grating, then cut the pieces at home and took them to the boat to assemble in the cockpit and make any necessary adjustments. Then I took them home and glued them together.

The next project was a cabin heater. I bought a small "Cole" stove that could burn wood or charcoal and mounted it on the bulkhead at the forward end of the starboard berth in the main cabin. The stove could be used like a fireplace with a sliding door open. I had to cut a large hole in the cabin top to install the stainless steel chimney and then make the penetration waterproof following the instructions that came with the stove.

Then I tackled the installations of a knotlog and depth sounder. This required cutting holes in the bottom of the boat with a hole saw, installing and sealing the two senders, and snaking the wires through the bilge and aft bulkhead to the location of the display units. Holes had to be cut in the bulkhead and the units installed and sealed.

The final project was to make a teak bracket for the compass, which would be mounted on the mizzenmast. The mount and the wiring for the compass light would be installed when the boat was rigged in the spring.

All the projects were completed in time for the launch in the spring, including painting the name on the transom. My ancestors had arrived in Halifax, Nova Scotia in 1751 on a boat named *Pearl*. They were German immigrants brought into the Nova Scotia by the British to populate the area after they had defeated the French. Since we would be sailing to Nova Scotia on the new boat we named it *Pearl II*. Just for fun we named the dinghy *Nit 1*.

On Saturday May 27th 1978 Jackie Stone drove Joyce, John, Tim, and me to Marblehead and dropped us off to pick up the boat and sail it to Marion. It had already been launched and rigged by Graves Yacht Yards except for the compass, which I installed. We thought the boat was beautiful in the water, but were disappointed to discover that the deck fill labeled "water" was only for the forward tank. There were two other water tanks under the berths in the main cabin, and they had to be filled by dragging a hose into the cabin and lifting off the cushions.

There were two fuel tanks, one under each cockpit seat. Since there were no fuel gages a sounding stick was used to determine the amount of fuel in each tank. After using the engine for a number of hours I discovered that the tank I thought we were using was still full. I checked the other tank and it was **not** full. The tank-selection switch had been mis-connected and pointed to the wrong tank.

Saturday was very foggy so we waited until Sunday to leave for Marion. Sunday morning it was still foggy, but we left Marblehead anyway. The fog lifted early and we had a beautiful sail to Scituate in a nice southwest breeze. We were well pleased with the way our new boat sailed.

We stayed overnight on a mooring in Scituate and got up at daybreak for an early start because we had 60 miles to cover. It was Memorial Day weekend and John had to be back at the Rhode Island School of Design the next day. It was a beautiful sunny day with a steady and favorable wind.

We reached the Cape Cod Canal in good time. The current was in our favor and we motored through. When we reached the Railroad Bridge we were in pea soup fog. We could hear behind us one of the container ships that had been waiting at the entrance to the canal when we entered. Its horn was bellowing and its motor roaring so we hugged the north shore to keep out of its way. Suddenly a little white outboard motor boat full of people came zipping out of the fog. One of them shouted, "Which way to Buzzards Bay?" We told them we were going to Buzzards Bay but if they meant the town rather than the bay it was back in the other direction. Off they zipped; no charts, no compass, and not knowing where they were in the fog!

Sailing *Pearl II* from Marblehead to Marion

After leaving the canal we motored from buoy to buoy along the Hog Island Channel. We didn't have a great deal of confidence in either the knot log or the depth sounder because neither one had been calibrated. The fog was still thick, and to make things worse it was getting dark. Just when we thought we were lost, can "5" on the route into Sippican Harbor (Marion) appeared out of the fog. We were right on course and easily found our way into the harbor and to our new mooring.

The previous summer Don Sullivan and Dick Stone had sold the *Scrimshaw*. Don bought another boat and named it *Idiot's Delight*. He put it on the mooring he had rented to us, so we thought we would be without a mooring. During the winter I had talked about my mooring problem to John Hughes, another sailor at Bolt Beranek and Newman. It turned out that John lived in a house right on Marion harbor, across from the town dock. He told me he owned two moorings out in the harbor in front of his house and that he would be happy to rent one to me at a nominal price. I readily accepted his offer and we used the mooring for the rest of our sailing days. It was across the harbor from the town dock and a long row, but it was always available. When we arrived at the mooring at the end of our trip from Marblehead there was a sign on the pickup stick that said, "Welcome Parker Hirtle".

We made several trips to Hadley Harbor in June, and in July we sailed to Cuttyhunk. There must have been a northwest wind since it is a painful trip beating to windward in the usual southwest wind in Buzzards Bay. Cuttyhunk pond was mobbed with boats so we motored through Canapitset Channel, a narrow, rocky passage between Cuttyhunk and Nashawena Islands, and sailed across Vineyard Sound to Menemsha Pond.

It was dead low tide when we left Menemsha Pond the next day and we ran aground in the entrance channel. A boy came along in an outboard motorboat with a big black engine and allowed as to how he would get us off in a jiffy. We tossed him the end of our main halyard. He cleated it and gunned his engine, heeling *Pearl II* and sliding us off sideways into deeper water. Joyce handed him a $5.00 bill and we were on our way. He puttered around the area waiting for the next careless sailor to run aground. On a later visit I explored the channel with a lead line and found that the deepest part of the channel was very close to a nun at the entrance, and that it was necessary to hug the nun except at high tide.

There were other weekend cruises in Buzzards Bay during July. The weekend of the 15th and 16th was overcast and unpleasant so rather than sailing I spent the time installing a radiotelephone, which Joyce had insisted on because of her father's declining health and her concern that he might take a turn for the worse at any time. I had made triangular plywood steps that fit in the slot in the mizzenmast. I slid them up the mast and climbed up and installed the antenna.

Parker up the Mast

10
TO MAINE ON *PEARL II*

When August 1978 came along it was time for a Maine cruise on *Pearl II*. Joyce was unable to leave when my vacation started for some reason that we don't remember. The solution was for me to sail single-handed to Falmouth Foreside. Joyce would drive there the day after I arrived and we would rendezvous to begin our cruise.

Joyce drove me to Marion the evening of August 1ˢᵗ and returned to Lexington. I slept on the boat and left Marion early the next morning, motored through the Cape Cod Canal, and sailed across Cape Cod Bay in pleasant weather to Provincetown. I anchored in the harbor and called Joyce to let her know I had arrived safely. Then I had dinner and turned in early – I had a long voyage to the Isles of Shoals ahead of me the next day.

Wood End Light* outside Provincetown

The weather was overcast in the morning and there was very little wind. I motored out past Long Point and Wood End lights to Race Point, where I set a course for White Island Light at the Isles of Shoals, due north at 55 miles. After a short time it started to rain–then it rained harder–then it became a downpour–it flooded the cockpit–it seeped through my foul weather gear–it soaked me to the skin–it went on hour after hour–I stood in the cockpit shouting at the sky! When the rain finally stopped a light breeze came up from the southwest. I put up the main, mizzen, and

---

*Lighthouse keepers were a dedicated lot. One foggy night the mechanism for the Long Point fog bell broke down. Timing himself with a watch the keeper pulled a rope to ring the 1,000 lb. bell every 30 seconds from 10:45 at night until 8 a.m. the next morning, when the fog finally dissipated.

genoa and sailed along nicely at a reasonable speed. When I was about 10 miles from the Isles of Shoals I realized that I would be arriving after dark. I hadn't taken into account the time it would take to get around long point on the way to the Race Point bell. As I got closer the wind began to increase and the sea became rough. I went forward on the lurching bow and managed, after a struggle, to get the genoa down and the working jib up. With this accomplished the ride became more civilized.

I passed to the west of White Island light in darkness. Soon the lights of the Oceanic Hotel appeared to starboard and I felt comfortable that I could find my way into Gosport Harbor with the aid of the hotel lights. When the bearing to the lights was approximately 125 degrees I would change course to 115 degrees, which should take me to the bell at the entrance to the harbor. But the hotel lights went out before it was time to turn! I thought there was a power failure and that I was in real trouble! After a few moments the lights came on again – then off – then on again. I breathed a sigh of relief after finally realizing that the lights hadn't gone out – they had been obscured by Lunging Island and then by Halfway Rocks. The remaining problem was that the compass was blurry and I couldn't read the numbers. By counting from the north arrow, which was quite prominent, I managed to get a bearing close enough to turn towards the bell at the proper time (See chart on page 170). I later learned that the compass visibility problem was caused by condensation on the glass dome, which I could have wiped off with my handkerchief. After passing the bell and entering Gosport Harbor I spotted to my starboard a white pole the size of a telephone pole standing about four feet above the water with a heavy pennant hanging from it. A mooring! I turned to windward towards the pole, sheeted the mizzen in tight, turned the main and jib sheets loose, drifted gently up to the mooring, and dropped the loop of the mooring pennant over the bow cleat. Once the pennant was cleated, I went down into the cabin to pour myself a hooker of scotch and call Joyce.

The last 50 miles the next day, from the Isles of Shoals to Falmouth Foreside, were uneventful and I arrived at Falmouth Foreside before dark, got a mooring from Handy Boat, had dinner at "The Galley", and turned in. The only problem was that I had backed down on the dinghy painter at the dock, and tangled it up in the prop.

Joyce arrived in the early afternoon and we celebrated our reunion by eating ice cream cones. We then motored over to the Portland Yacht Club dock, where there was a diver. I asked him to cut the dinghy painter from the prop and check the knot log paddle wheel because the knot log was not working properly. When he came up he said he knocked off a large barnacle from in front of the paddle wheel. We expected that the bottom must be covered with barnacles because the boat did not seem to be sailing as fast as it did when we sailed from Marblehead to Marion. It had been in the showroom for at least six months before launching and Graves had not repainted the bottom. In those days bottom paint lost its effectiveness after only a few days out of the water. When *Pearl II* was hauled in the fall our suspicions were confirmed – the bottom was covered with barnacles.

Handy Boat at Falmouth Foreside

In late afternoon we sailed over to Jewel Island and anchored in the cove. We retraced the route in reverse that John and I had taken from Jewel to Falmouth Foreside on *Snoopy* several years before, but this time there was no fog and the visibility was excellent. I was interested in seeing the passage through Chandler Cove, which was the trickiest part of our trip in the fog (see chart on page 18). In the morning, after breakfast, Joyce and I

The Punchbowl at Jewel Island

took a short walk across the island to the punchbowl and then departed for Boothbay, a distance of 24 miles.

We found a place to anchor in Boothbay Harbor and went ashore. The harbor is large and the shore is densely populated with commercial venues of all kinds; restaurants, shops, marine facilities, etc. We went ashore and had dinner in a restaurant with a great view of the harbor: Although the dinner and view were good, we decided that Boothbay was not our kind of place, and that we wouldn't make an effort to return any time in the future.

Boothbay Harbor

The next day we visited the Grand Banks Schooner Museum. The schooner on display, the *Sherman Zwicker*, was built at the Smith & Rhuland Shipyard in Lunenburg, Nova Scotia, the same yard that had built the famous *Bluenose* and *Bluenose II*. The *Sherman Zwicker* had short masts and was equipped with a large marine diesel engine and engine-driven auxiliary equipment. This was a disappointment because we had expected to see a traditional Grand Banks fishing schooner built when they operated under sail only and when everything was done by hand.

From Boothbay we sailed through Fisherman Island Passage, past Pemaquid Point and up Muscongus Sound to Round Pond, where we picked up a mooring. We went ashore and called our friends Paul and Maria Duggan, who had moved from Lexington to Chamberlin, Maine. They came to Round Pond and invited us to their house to take a shower and spend the night. From then on we made a special effort to see Paul and Maria on our Maine cruises, frequently meeting them for dinner at the Coveside Restaurant at Christmas Cove.

The next day we went up to the north of Hog Island in Muscongus bay to see a derelict three-masted schooner (see footnote on page 43). From there it was on to Friendship, where we went ashore to buy supplies and visit the tiny Friendship Museum. Although Friendship Harbor is large and has many moorings and boats, unlike Boothbay it is quiet and peaceful and is not surrounded by commercial activities. The center of town is a short walk from the harbor. After having visited several new harbors we were anxious to get to get to McGlathery Island again, a distance of about 40 miles. The weather was good and the wind was light from the Southwest.

Derelict Schooner

Friendship Harbor

We were learning that this was a common wind pattern on the Maine coast. We sailed and motored off and on and anchored in the cove in late afternoon. It was near low tide and I went clamming for the first time. We didn't have a clam hoe or anything else I could dig with, so I found a flat stone and used it for a clam hoe. My efforts were successful and we hung the clams over the side in a string bag. The next day we made a delicious clam chowder, which we had for lunch with sandwiches. The weather stayed nice, and as usual we stayed at McGlathery for several days just walking the beach, reading, and relaxing.

Friendship Museum

Clamming with a Flat Stone

We left McGlathery and headed back west, ending up at Tenants Harbor where we picked up a Cod End mooring. We went ashore for supplies at Cod End and the local store and then stopped at the big white house that had been converted to an inn and restaurant since our last visit. It was now the "East Wind Inn". We made reservations for dinner and returned later for drinks and an excellent fish dinner, seated at a table that overlooked the harbor. The East Wind Inn was a great addition to Tenants Harbor and we returned there many times in the following years and were never disap-pointed with the food and drinks, the service, and the overall ambience of the place. On one of our visits we even rented a room for the night, slept ashore, and then had breakfast in the dining room.

View from East Wind Inn Dining Room

We left in the morning and tacked against a southwest wind to Georges Harbor, a narrow slit between Allen and Benner Islands in the southeast corner of Muscongus Bay. We anchored and went ashore to explore the island and the old uninhabited houses on Allen Island.

Old Houses on Allen Island

From Georges Harbor we crossed Muscongus Bay to New Harbor, a snug fishing harbor on the east side of Pemaquid Neck. This was a real fishing harbor, lined on the north side with floats used for the fishing operations. We landed at one of the fishing docks to inquire about a mooring and almost fell into a big opening in the dock, apparently there for holding lobsters. We got a mooring and then rowed ashore to one of the floats and walked around to explore the north shore of the harbor, where all the activity took place.

There was a steep bank up from the harbor, and many of the fishing facilities were entered at the second level. In our wandering around we found a place on the upper level that served lobster dinners and we dined on an open deck with a great view of the harbor.

New Harbor

From New Harbor we stopped in at Five Islands for supplies and then went on to the harbor at Cape Newagen, where we anchored for the night. The harbor was quiet when we turned in but uncomfortable rolling of the boat awakened us during the night. The tide had risen and swells were coming in over the reefs to the south that formed the harbor. This is a nice harbor when the tide is low and the reefs form a good barrier, but when the tide is high it is hardly a harbor at all. An overnight stay is inadvisable unless the tide will be low in the middle of the night so the reefs form a suitable barrier against the sea.

After a restless night we headed west again and went far up in Quahog Bay. We anchored and spent the night in a quiet, peaceful anchorage to the east of Snow Island. It was quite a contrast to Newagen. There were no other boats there and no activity on the shore. During a visit several years later it seemed like an entirely different place, with a lot of boats and tents and noisy activity on the water and on the land. We witnessed this happening in many locations in Maine and Massachusetts during our cruising years.

Pearl II at Quiet Anchorage in Quahog Bay

From Quahog Bay it was back to Falmouth Foreside. We motored in to the dock at Handy Boat and rented a mooring for a week. I lashed the dinghy on deck and motored out to the mooring, then took the launch ashore and we drove home to Lexington. The cruise was a good test for *Pearl II*. We were really pleased with the comfort of the accommodations and with her performance under sail, although she was not as fast as when we sailed from Marblehead to Marion because of barnacles.

Motoring to the Mooring at Falmouth Foreside

I had arranged to get a ride back to Falmouth Foreside with Lexington friends Pete and Nancy Engels, who kept their boat there. The next weekend John and I rode back with Pete and Nancy and sailed *Pearl II* back to Marion.

Although there were no major cruises during the summer of 1979, Joyce and I did go to Nantucket for a few days. One evening at Nantucket we had a memorable dinner downstairs at "Obedia's", a restaurant that had been highly recommended to us. We had drinks before dinner, a bottle of wine with our meal, and Dutch and Irish coffee after dinner on an outdoor patio upstairs, in pleasant evening weather. It was a delightful experience over all. By the time we were ready to leave we were somewhat tipsy, to say the least. We stumbled around in the dark and managed to get back to the dock, after stopping for a while for Joyce to rest, leaning on the hood of a car. Somehow we were able to get down to the float, into the dinghy, and back onto the boat without capsizing or falling in. Neither of us has ever had that much to drink, and with such debilitating effect, either before or after Obedia's.

While we were at Nantucket the brig *Unicorn* came in and anchored. We had seen the *Unicorn* at the tall ships parade and at the dock afterwards. I was amazed at the number of lines coming down the masts and coiled at the bottom, and finally understood where the phrase "learning the ropes" came from. What looked like a tangle of lines had to be carefully planned and arranged for ready access, and the crew had to learn the location and purpose of every one of the lines, in order to respond quickly to the bosn's commands.

The Brig Unicorn   "Learning the Ropes"

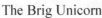

Another adventure to remember occurred on a trip to Lake Tashmoo on Martha's Vineyard. The trip was uneventful until we left Tashmoo. We had planned to go through Woods Hole at slack tide, since the current in the hole was too strong and turbulent at other times. We couldn't start the engine when it was time to leave – the starter was dead. The wind was light from the southwest. We sailed out through the narrow entrance channel and across vineyard Sound to Woods Hole. To our surprise and delight, the water in Woods Hole was like a millpond – not a ripple! We ghosted through the hole and went in to Hadley Harbor for the night. We hadn't thought the water in Woods Hole could ever be that tranquil. Every other time we had gone through, the water had been rough and swirling around in all directions, even at or near slack tide.

Early in the summer of 1979 there was another Tall Ships Parade in Boston and we went again. This time we took along John's current girlfriend, Tracy, whom he had met at the Rhode Island School of Design. The parade was just about the same as the one we had attended in 1976 on the *Anemone*, but not quite as exciting the second time.

Watching the Tall Ships Parade

There were several short cruises in the summer of 1980, including trips to Hadley Harbor and Tarpaulin Cove. Late in July Joyce and I took a weekend cruise through the canal and across Cape Cod Bay to Provincetown. We had planned to rendezvous in Provincetown Harbor with Ed and Martha Roney, members of the Charles River Power Squadron. On the way to Provincetown the wind in Cape Cod Bay was southwest at 15-20 knots and we made a fast passage with Joyce at the wheel for part of the way and Uncle Otto steering for the rest of the way. (Uncle Otto was a below-decks autopilot that I installed at the beginning of the boating season in anticipation of our upcoming Nova Scotia cruise.) When we met the Roneys they said they had a wild and wet trip in their wooden powerboat.

Joyce Steering to Provincetown

Uncle Otto Steering to Provincetown

The passage from the end of the canal to Provincetown was the high point of the weekend for us.

11

A NOVA SCOTIA CRUISE ON *PEARL II*

After a few short cruises in 1980 it was time to take Pearl II to Nova Scotia. We planned to go to the Race Point buoy off the tip of Cape Cod and then offshore to the Brazil Rock buoy, a common destination for boats cruising to Nova Scotia. The distance from Race Point to Brazil Rock would be about 227 miles and the total distance from Marion to LaHave, Nova Scotia would be about 325 miles. I didn't relish the idea of steering for 227 miles offshore so I had installed a below-decks autopilot at the beginning of the season. Once the course was set "Uncle Otto" could be turned off and then on again without the course being changed. We were well equipped for the voyage. We had a good compass, a depth sounder, a knotlog, a radio direction finder (RDF), a radiotelephone, a sextant, a Hewlett Packard calculator with a sun-sight program, and all the necessary charts. Although loran was then available it was somewhat complicated to use. We would go without one and wait for a simpler unit with the capability of conversion to latitude and longitude.

On the morning of Sunday August 3rd 1980 Joyce, Tim, and I boarded *Pearl II* in Marion after a champagne sendoff and dinner at Carbo's Restaurant in Wareham the night before. Present for the sendoff were Joyce's Sister Marjorie and her husband Garf, their daughter Martha and her husband Jack Rowe, and our son John, who had other commitments and couldn't make the trip. We sailed over to the Hog Island Channel and entered the Cape Cod Canal with a favorable wind and current. We moved along at about 8 knots under both sail and power. About half way through the canal the engine began to make a strange noise and smell. I was about to turn it off when I realized that it might not restart, and it is illegal to go through the canal under sail alone.

At the east end of the canal we motored in to the Harbor of Refuge, anchored, and turned off the engine. (Since then a large number of slips have been installed in the harbor, the name has been changed to the "Boat Basin", and there is no more anchoring.) The starter was dead and the engine could not be restarted. The ignition key, which operated just like an automobile ignition key, had not released and the starter had stayed engaged and burned up because of the high speed at which it was being rotated by the engine! It was Sunday and nothing could be done.

Monday morning I called Burr Brothers, a Cape Dory dealer in Marion, and explained what had happened. I thought they would have a starter in stock since ours had burned out in Lake Tashmoo the previous year and when they replaced it they said they had to replace three others that year.

Burr Brothers did not have a starter but they would order one from Yanmar in New Jersey. It should be in by Tuesday or Wednesday, and I should call about noon since their shipments arrived in the late morning.

Tuesday morning we saw a thick plume of black smoke to the west, then black soot began to rain down on the boat. One of the huge oil tanks of the Canal Electric Company, holding nearly 6 million gallons of oil, had caught fire and exploded. This was unpleasant, but even worse, Tuesday at noon there was **no starter**! And Wednesday there was **no starter**!

The Plume of Smoke Drifting over the Harbor of Refuge

I called Yanmar in New Jersey and they said they had shipped it, but Thursday there still was **no starter**! When I called Burr Brothers their explanation was that UPS must have lost the shipment. I cussed out the Burr Brothers person on the phone, waited to cool down a little, and then called Andy Vavolotis, the president of Cape Dory Yachts. I told him our story and that we were wasting my three-week vacation imprisoned at the

Harbor of Refuge. He was very sympathetic, kept saying, "Oh my" and thought they might have one in the factory on a Cape Dory 27. He went to check but returned to say no luck. He would try to locate one and I should call him back at 3:00 PM. When I called him back he said he had located a starter and that mechanics from Burr Brothers would be there to install it at 6:00, and God help them if they didn't show up! Two mechanics did show up at 5:55 and installed the new starter in 20 minutes. They said Vavolotis had located it on a crated engine in New Bedford and had it removed and driven to Marion!

I had spent a lot of the time while we were held up doing odd jobs around the boat, including taking the head apart and sealing all the joints and cracks that had been leaking. That afternoon Joyce and Tim had gone ashore and bought a pound and a half of swordfish and three blocks of ice. After the mechanics left I poured us drinks: a martini on the rocks for me, Scotch on the rocks for Joyce, and root beer for Tim. Then we dined on swordfish, potatoes, and 3-bean salad. After dinner I decided we had wasted enough time and that we should leave as soon as we got everything shipshape. We got everything organized below, I lashed the dinghy on deck, and we motored in to the dock to get water. The dock hose had been stored away for the night and we had to fill the tanks by many trips lugging water in five-gallon plastic containers. (I later bought a flat hose on a reel to keep on the boat for such occasions.) When the tanks were full we motored out and passed the red flasher at the end of the canal at 11:20. We finally were on our way!

There wasn't much wind and we motored for two hours, then put up the sails. We were at the Race Point buoy at 2:55 Friday morning and set Uncle Otto on a course to Brazil Rock, 227 miles away (see chart on pages iv and v). Joyce and Tim went to bed and I stayed up for the night to check on Uncle Otto and to keep a watch for other boats. Joyce got up at dawn and took over. We were heading easterly so the sun rose almost dead ahead. The sky turned red-orange then rosy pink. A large ketch appeared ahead motoring on a reciprocal course to ours with its sails flapping. It made quite a picture with the red sky as a background, but we failed to take a picture. The only other boat we saw on Friday was a huge freighter heading in to Portland. When the sun came up we were sailing straight into an almost blinding light until it rose well above the horizon. There was nothing out there but huge swells that we rode up and down over easily. Tim, who was prone to seasickness, took his Dramamine faithfully and spent most of the time in his bunk.

In the afternoon I used my sextant to take two sets of sun sights about four hours apart and got a running fix. Each set of sights provides a line of position and by advancing the first line by the distance on the log, two crossing lines are obtained on the chart, indicating the present position.

Freighter Heading For Portland

The fix indicated that we were several miles off course, so we adjusted Uncle Otto accordingly.

Joyce found preparing meals to be a trial and had no appetite for the hamburger stew she cooked up for dinner. Instead she ate a jelly sandwich, exclaiming that it would have been a good idea to make up a bunch of sandwiches beforehand and keep them in the icebox to eat during the day. She found it difficult to "mess with food" when everything was lurching around in a totally unpredictable fashion.

Joyce Steering to Nova Scotia

I spent Friday night in the cockpit napping and occasionally rising to look around for the lights of any boats that might happen by. None did.

Saturday the sky was overcast and the wind was from the southwest at about 15 knots. Huge waves were coming at us from the starboard quarter; Uncle Otto was not able to respond quickly enough so Joyce and I took turns steering. Joyce said great walls of water were rising behind me when I was steering. Petrels were gliding along in the troughs and porpoises were playing around the bow and occasionally dashing under the bow to the other side. The whole scene was awesome. Tim slept through it all, waking up only for meals and Dramamine. Late in the afternoon I got out the RDF and located a signal from the radio beacon on Seal Island at the southern tip of Nova Scotia. It was comforting to know we were not on our way to Ireland. Hopefully the next thing we would see would be the red flashing buoy at Brazil Rock.

Brazil Rock Buoy

What we thought was the Brazil Rock buoy appeared as we had hoped – dead ahead! When we got close, however, there was no name or number on the buoy. Nothing! I didn't think it could be such an important marker, since it had no identification on it. I assumed it was another less important buoy that was nearby on the chart, and changed our course based on this assumption. After a short time, however, I changed my mind and concluded that it **was** the Brazil Rock buoy and that it had recently been replaced with a temporary one with no identification on it. So we turned back towards the unmarked buoy. By the time we reached it darkness had set in, and with my fingers crossed I set a course for Shelburne Harbor, which was to be our landfall. My guess was correct and we reached the buoy at the entrance to Shelburne Harbor at daybreak and motored in to the dock. The dock was crowded with fishing boats and one small sailboat that appeared to have arrived from offshore and was rafted up to one of them.

Pearl II at Shelburne Harbor

We rafted up to one of the smaller fishing boats and I went ashore to find a telephone and call my cousin Greta at Petite Reviere to let her know we had arrived. Greta and her husband, Lawrence Himmelman, arrived several hours later. Lawrence suggested that Joyce and Tim could drive to Petite Reviere with Greta, and he would sail to LaHave with me. Joyce would have none of this. She said, "No way! I didn't come all this way across the ocean to miss a nice sail along the Nova Scotia coast". So Greta, Lawrence, and Tim, who was happy to be off the boat, drove to Petite Reviere, and Joyce and I took a long nap before dinner and then went to bed early. We had to sail more than 70 miles to get to LaHave the next day.

We were up at the crack of dawn in the morning. The weather was beautiful with a 10 to 15 knot southwesterly breeze, and we were looking forward to a good sail to LaHave. The wind and weather were just about perfect for the entire day and we spent most of the time with our backs against the cabin bulkhead watching the wake, while Uncle Otto steered. We occasionally went below for drinks and sandwiches. The rest of the time we kept our watch on the wake astern. The sail along the coast was a truly memorable one – perfect weather and wind and not another boat to be seen for the entire 70 miles. This could never happen in New England waters, even on the Maine coast. All the offshore buoys had names painted prominently on them, reinforcing my thought that the Brazil Rock Buoy was a temporary one.

Shelburne Harbor in the Morning

Late in the day we passed the lighthouse on Mosher's Head at the mouth of the LaHave River and at 6:00 PM we tied up at the Himmelman dock in LaHave. We were greeted at the dock by Greta, Lawrence, Tim, and my mother, who was visiting "down home" for several weeks.

Mosher's Head Lighthouse at the Mouth of the LaHave River

While in Nova Scotia we stayed with Greta and Lawrence in their farmhouse at Petite Reviere. The day after we arrived Lawrence called the customs inspector. He appeared later in the day and came aboard *Pearl II*. During his brief inspection he asked if we had any liquor aboard. I said we did and showed him the open bottles. He said, "Well, you'll drink those up yourselves while you're here, so they're not a problem".

During our time in Nova Scotia we took several short trips on the LaHave River and up the coast. One day we motored across the river and anchored at Middle LaHave to visit my cousin Beulah's husband Charles Walters. Beulah had died several years before. My father had been the youngest of five children so most of my cousins were older than I was, and they were beginning to die off. While at Middle LaHave I took pictures of

The Hirtle Homestead

St. Marks Church

grand-father Hirtle's house, where I was born, and the adjacent church, St. Marks. My great grandfather Benjamin Hirtle donated the land for the church, and my grandfather Henry added to the church property. My cousin Beulah had been the organist for many years, and Henry's five children, including my father, donated the money for a new church organ.

Pearl II anchored at Middle LaHave

Charles escorted *Pearl II* down the river in his outboard motorboat to visit another cousin, Donny Corkum. Donny's son, Rodney said that he wouldn't have considered making the voyage we did without loran.

Another short trip was an overnight to Mahone Bay with Greta and Lawrence. He was the president of the "OK Service", which was founded by his father and had been trading with Caribbean islands for many years. They imported all the rum that came in to the Maritimes. When we were there they also were importing dynamite, which was stored in a facility at Mahone Bay before distribution. At Mahone Bay we went by Hirtle Cove and the dynamite storage site, anchored, and cooked a steak on our charcoal grille.

The Town of Mahone Bay

Hirtle Cove

One day I took my mother on Pearl II for a 10-mile trip up the LaHave River to Bridgewater. She had made this trip many times years ago with my father on his boat, the *Mystery*, to go to the movies. She had told me about those trips, and I was sure she would enjoy a repeat performance after so many years. The weather was pleasant, warm and sunny, and the trip was a great success. I was amazed at the number of small churches along both sides of the river between LaHave and Bridgewater. The German protestant immigrants must have been a highly religious group.

Small Churches along LaHave River

Our longest cruise in Nova Scotia was to Rogue's Roost, which was more than 30 miles from the LaHave River, near Halifax. There were no other boats in this secluded, well-protected anchorage. Unfortunately the weather was cloudy and overcast, so we were not able to enjoy it as much as we would have if it had been sunny and pleasant.

Pearl II Anchored at Rogues Roost

While we were in Nova Scotia the LaHave people threw a big birthday party for Ernie Himmelman, Lawrence's father. It was held on a beautiful sunny day in a stockade behind the Petite Reviere farmhouse. The stockade had been built to allow outdoor activities, such as this one, to be carried out in comfort even on windy days.

Ernie Himmelman's Birthday Party

We stayed in Nova Scotia for about a week before heading back to Massachusetts. We had planned to stay longer, but didn't have as much time as we thought we would because of the delay in the Harbor of Refuge due to the starter problem. Our plan for the return trip to Marion was to sail down the Nova Scotia coast the first day and put in at a convenient port for the night. We would then make an overnight passage to Mt. Desert Rock and then proceed to a port in Maine, where we would stay for the second night. From there we would make day trips down the coast.

We left the Himmelman dock in LaHave at 7:30 AM on Wednesday the 20th of August. Just outside the LaHave River there was a Canadian Coast Guard vessel changing a buoy. Maybe they would go to Brazil Rock and put in a proper buoy there. We had a long sail that day, passing Shelburne and continuing 13 miles to Port LaTour, where we anchored for the night.

Leaving LaHave

Canadian Coast Guard

We left Port LaTour at 8:10 in the morning with an east wind of 10 to 15 knots, passed Cape Sable at 12:05 and the Blonde Rock buoy at 2:24 PM. From Blonde Rock we headed across the Gulf of Maine. I had checked the schedule of the Yarmouth to Bar Harbor ferry and concluded that our courses would intersect sometime in the night and that we had better keep a close watch to avoid being run down. The distance to Mt. Desert Rock was about 90 miles. At an average speed of five knots we should arrive there between eight and nine the next morning. We did see the ferry lights sometime after midnight, but we were not on a collision course and there was no danger.

Mt. Desert Rock

We passed Mt. Desert Rock at 8:00 the next morning, having averaged just a bit over 5 knots from Blonde Rock. By this time the wind had shifted to the northeast at 15 knots. This was a favorable wind for sailing to McGlathery Island, which would take between five and six hours at the speed we had averaged from Blonde Rock, so McGlathery was our destination for the day. Our arrival time at McGlathery was 1:15 PM. After two and a half days of almost continuous sailing from LaHave we relaxed at McGlathery Island for the rest of the day

Saturday we stopped at Stonington for supplies and then sailed across Isle au Haut Bay to the south of Vinalhaven Island. On the way we passed Mark Island light, one of the prettiest little lighthouses on the coast.

Mark Island Light

This was a slow trip, since the wind had shifted to southwest, just the way we were going, and we had to tack all the way. From there it was across West Penobscot Bay to Hewett Island at the south end of Muscle Ridge Channel, where we anchored in a cove on the south side of the island (see chart on page 211). The cove was well protected from the south and west by surrounding islands. After dinner a teenage boy came by in an outboard motorboat and stopped to chat. We invited him aboard and he stayed for several hours. He and his parents were there for the summer, and he seemed to be bored silly. Both parents went lobster fishing in small boats, his mother's being an outboard. He said his mother always caught more lobsters than his father did. The next morning we met his mother while he was preparing lobster bait with her.

We left Hewitt Island at 5:50 AM to go to Christmas Cove. There were heavy swells and the wind was light and variable. We sailed whenever we could and motored the rest of the time, arriving at Christmas cove at 4:40

PM. Our average speed to Christmas Cove was only 3-1/2 knots. We got a mooring and went ashore for drinks and a good fish dinner at the Coveside Restaurant. Christmas Cove had become one of our favorite harbors and we often stopped there to have dinner.

Preparing Lobster Bait at Hewett Island

When we left Christmas Cove the next morning the wind was still light and variable. We sailed and motored to Jewel Island and anchored in the cove at about 5:00 PM.

Portland LNB

Tuesday August 25th we sailed to Gosport Harbor, at the Isles of Shoals, passing the Portland Large Navigational Buoy (LNB). The Portland LNB replaced the lightship that had been moored at that location for many years. The buoy is instrumented to measure wind speed, wave heights, and other meteorological information, and automatically transmits the data to a shore station by radio.

The next day we sailed to Gloucester and got a mooring behind the breakwater. The mooring was comfortable for the night, but in the early morning we were rocked awake by fishing boats motoring out of the inner harbor. We got up and dressed, and then made pancakes for breakfast. During breakfast Joyce's plate full of pancakes and syrup was thrown from the table onto the cabin sole by waves from the fishing boats.

We had a favorable east wind of 10 to 20 knots from Gloucester to Provincetown. It was cloudy and overcast, but to compensate for the unpleasant weather we averaged almost 6-1/2 knots for the day's sail.

The Provincetown Fishing Fleet   The Burned Oil Tank (in the Center)

Friday August 29th we sailed from Provincetown to the Cape Cod Canal. After entering the canal we passed the oil tanks and saw the one that had burned while we were stuck in the Harbor of Refuge at the beginning of our cruise. We motored through the canal, sailed down Buzzards Bay and completed our trip from LaHave by picking up our mooring in Marion Harbor. It was a great cruise except for the beginning when we were delayed in the Harbor of Refuge. Now we had two days to recover before heading back to work on Monday morning.

12
PEARL II – 1981

Early in 1981 I read an article in one of the boating magazines about designing and installing a "mule" sail on a Seawind ketch. The mule is a sail that fills the triangular area between the main and mizzen sails. I was intrigued and thought that *Pearl II* should have a mule, so I gave Steve Sperry of Sperry Sails in Marion the dimensions of the sail I wanted. He said he had never made a mule, but he would give it his best shot. He had the sail ready in the spring and after *Pearl II* was launched I added a new stay and halyard for the sail. The first tryout was a total failure. The sail acted like a bag. Then I realized that the sail in the article I had read had a half-wishbone to make the sail set properly, so I fashioned and installed a half wishbone of aluminum tubing. The mule worked beautifully. *Pearl II* now had four self-tacking sails: a club-footed jib, main, mizzen, and mule. There was only one problem with the mule – it was difficult to set and furl – I had to stand on the afterdeck and stretch up as far as I could to reach it.

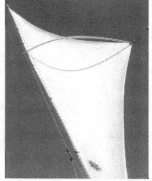

Pearl II with Four Self-tacking Sails   The Mule

There were weekend cruises on *Pearl II* during June and July, including Hadley Harbor and Cuttyhunk.

On Monday August 2nd 1981 Joyce and I were off to Maine again. We planned to visit favorite harbors and anchorages and some new ones as well. Since it would now take three days to sail to Maine if we stopped at night, we made an overnight passage to allow more time in Maine. It was a clear sunny day. We left Marion at 9:00 AM and sailed to Race Point, where we set a course for the Manana whistle with the wind astern at 10 knots. In the middle of the night we were dodging fishing boat lights on Jeffreys

Ledge, a problem we had on many overnight passages. Tuesday morning we were motoring in fog. At 2:45 PM we turned off the engine to hear the Manana whistle and then changed our course for Georges Harbor, where we anchored at 5:45. Georges Harbor was full of lobster pot buoys.

We stayed until 11:00 the next morning. When I tried to pull up the anchor it wouldn't budge, so I started the engine, put it in gear, and bang! a lobster pot warp wrapped around the propeller and stopped the engine. I put on my swim trunks and went over the side in the frigid water to try to free the propeller, but was unable to figure out the tangle of lines around the propeller, including our anchor rode. (I loved to dive off the boat and swim at Tarpaulin Cove and some of the Buzzards Bay anchorages, but I only went in the frigid Maine waters when I had to.) Fortunately, a lobster boat came along and the lobsterman saw our plight. He pulled up the lines, untangled them, cut some and tied them together, and we were free. There still was a line wrapped around the propeller, but it was not fastened to anything. The lobsterman said he would be back later and would tow us to Friendship if we couldn't free the propeller. After he left I went over the side again with a sharp knife and easily cut the lines off. Lobster pot buoys and warps are a serious problem for cruising boats in the Maine waters when under power. The lobster boats have cages around their propellers, so they don't have the same problem.

From Georges Harbor we motored to Tenants Harbor in thick fog (visibility one boat length). We bought fish at Cod End for the next day and had dinner at the East Wind Inn. We found the food to be excellent, as it was on our previous visit. The next day was thick fog again so we stayed put for the day. There was a thunderstorm that night.

The next stop was a cozy anchorage between Cedar and Lawrys islands on the west side of Vinalhaven Island. There was fog and rain all the way to the anchorage. In addition, Uncle Otto got tired and quit steering, so we had to take over and steer. After we anchored many large sailboats came in and anchored and the occupants rowed ashore to a dock on Lawrys Island. Most of the people acted snooty as they rowed by and didn't acknowledge our presence. One middle-aged couple was an exception. As they rowed by they stopped and said hello and told us they were going to a party to celebrate the anniversary of the island's owner buying the island. They had been the brokers for the sale.

The next day the weather had cleared up but there was no wind. We motored to Northhaven for supplies and then sailed to McGlathery Island. It was a bit foggy at McGlathery, but not unpleasant. I worked on Uncle Otto and found and repaired a loose connection.

In the morning it was sunny and pleasant. I went ashore and dug clams, this time with an appropriate utensil, and we made clam chowder. I also collected wood for our little stove. A wood fire was cheery on cool, foggy

Joyce – Happy to be back   Rock at McGlathery Island

days, but it deposited a lot of ash on the deck. We eventually gave up wood and switched to charcoal; it burned cleaner and gave off more heat.

We stayed at McGlathery for another night and motored out in the morning. We arrived at Northeast Harbor at 3:00 PM, having motored in fog all the way. At Northeast Harbor we took showers in the Yachtsman Building, and then went shopping at the Pine Tree Market.

Tuesday August 11th was thick fog again so it was a lay day at Northeast Harbor. Wednesday we motored to the dock and got diesel fuel, water, and ice. Then we headed for Burnt Island Thorofare, where we found our way in past the notorious big rock and anchored. There was some fog, some sun, and not much wind, so we motored most of the way. The next day we went back to Tenants Harbor, arriving just in time to buy lobsters at Cod End.

The Yachtsman Building at Northeast Harbor

For some reason we didn't make an overnight trip on the way home to Marion; instead, we day-tripped down the coast. Overnight stops were made at Newagen, Jewel Island, and Provincetown.

We sailed all the way from Tenants Harbor to Newagen, making many sail changes because of the varying wind conditions. The harbor was calm for sleeping since low tide was in the middle of the night and no swells came in over the reefs. The sail to Jewel Island was mostly in rain and fog and the passage from there to Provincetown was a hairy one. The wind went from southwest to west and increased in velocity. We started out with all working sails and reduced sail each time our speed reached seven knots; first reefing the main, then dropping the main, then dropping the mizzen. We ended up doing 6-1/2 knots under the jib only. Sometime in the morning I looked back and *Nit 1* was not there! I pulled in the painter and there was nothing on it but the bow fitting, a small piece of plywood, and a ¾" wood backing piece that had been torn out of the bow. *Nit 1* must have flipped over in the storm and been torn loose. This was a great loss and we never towed a dinghy on our passages to and from Maine after this.

From Provincetown to the canal the weather was sunny and the wind was northwest at 10 to 20 knots, but when we got to Buzzards Bay the wind was light and from the south We arrived in Marion at 3:15 PM on Tuesday August 18th in sunshine. A beautiful day and a good sail!

Unfortunately we were now without a dinghy. I decided to make a temporary one out of ¼" exterior grade plywood. The first design was a total failure, but after extensive modifications it turned out to be a very practical solution to our dinghy problem (see Dinghy No.3, Chapter 24, pages 238 and 239).

13

NARRAGANSET BAY AND BLOCK ISLAND

During June and July of 1982 we made a number of weekend cruises in Buzzards Bay and one to Nantucket. In August we thought it was time for a change, so we would be going to Narragansett Bay rather than Maine for our long cruise. Tim would be going on this cruise with Joyce and me.

The first day of the Narragansett Bay cruise, Tuesday August 10th. was not a pleasant one. It was overcast and we tacked and motored into a light southwest wind, the prevailing wind direction on Buzzards Bay. When we passed Gooseberry Neck we had had enough, so we motored up the West-port River and anchored among the boats that were moored there. The next day was no better. The wind was still from the southwest, the weather was overcast, and there were swells causing the boat to roll. We arrived at Mackerel Cove on Conanicut Island near the entrance to Narragansett Bay at 5:00 PM and anchored in 14 feet of water. The boat rolled uncomfortably so I put out a stern anchor to keep it heading into the swells. It rained at night.

Breakfast in the morning was fried eggs, Spam, beans, toast, and coffee (the best part of the trip so far). The wind was northeast in the early afternoon and we sailed on a beam reach to Newport Harbor, where we got a mooring from Old Port Marine. We took the launch ashore and had bloody marys and chowder at the "Black Pearl", then walked around town and picked up some supplies before going back to the boat. It was cloudy all day.

Pearl II at Newport

Friday August 13th dawned sunny – at last! We hung around and went to J.T.Connel for some odds and ends of marine hardware I needed. It was a fantastic store with more marine stuff than I had ever seen. We then had a good dinner at the Black Pearl.

The next day was nice and sunny again. We took our time and sailed across East Passage to Potter Cove in fluky wind. Potter Cove was so full of powerboats that we renamed it "Stinkpotter Cove". This was seventh heaven for Tim, who loved powerboats, so we stayed the entire next day.

"Stinkpotter" Cove

Tim rowed around the cove looking at powerboats through his monocular. He came back from one of his excursions and reported an unpleasant episode with the occupants of one of the powerboats who accused him of spying on them. I rowed down the cove to the boat with Tim, and explained to them that he was not spying on them, that he was legally blind, that he loved powerboats, and that he was using a monocular to see them better. Having heard this, their attitude changed and they invited Tim aboard to tour their boat, which absolutely delighted him.

Monday August 16th was another beautiful sunny day. We reached across the bay to Bristol in the afternoon, tied up at the town dock, and went ashore to pick up some supplies. We also planned to do our laundry, but there was a sign on the Laundromat door, "Closed. Gone fishin". The dock was dirty and in need of repair and the area around it looked poor and depressed.

Tuesday was another nice day. We sailed west to East Greenwich and rented a slip at Norton Marine, the only time *Pearl II* was ever at a slip. It was an interesting experience to spend part of the day and a night able to go ashore by just walking off the boat. We stepped off the boat and walked a mile to the laundry, washed and dried our clothes, and walked a mile back. We were caught in a thunderstorm before we reached the dock. After changing into dry clothes we had dinner at the "Harborside Lobstermania".

Pearl II at a Slip at East Greenwich

Wednesday there was a light northeast wind. We sailed down East Passage under genoa, main, and mizzen. We turned west at the bottom of Narragansett Bay and went into the Point Judith Harbor of Refuge. The harbor was manmade by extensive breakwater construction at the southeast side of Point Judith. We went up The Breachway towards Snug Harbor but didn't stay there because of the strong current; we went back to the Harbor of Refuge and anchored in the south corner of the harbor close to the breakwater. We spent a comfortable night but were rolling in the morning at six o'clock when fishing boats left the harbor.

The wind was light from the west and then the southwest as we sailed south to Block Island, arriving in the Great Salt Pond in the early afternoon. We went ashore and had dinner at "Dead Eye Dick's".

We left Block Island the next morning at nine. The wind was westsouthwest at 15 knots and we had a wild ride past the Buzzards Bay tower to Cuttyhunk. The anchor was down in the Cuttyhunk Pond at 4:00 PM.

On Saturday morning August 21st we headed back to Marion. The wind was right on the nose, northeast at 15 knots. How we wished for the usual southwest wind, which we had when going in the other direction. Bad luck with the wind, both coming and going. We picked up our mooring in Marion at 4:30 PM after tacking back and forth all day under working sails and reefed main. The only saving grace was the self-tacking sails, so we didn't have to mess with the sheets on every tack.

A Wild Ride – Other Boats near the Buzzards Bay Tower

14
PEARL III

During February 1983 Joyce and I went to the Boston boat show. We weren't on the market for a boat, we just liked going to boat shows and looking at boats. Before that I had the opportunity to go to the Annapolis in-the-water boat show when on a business trip. I had seen and boarded a Crealock 37, built by Pacific Seacraft in Fullerton, California, and thought it was my kind of boat. It was available as a sloop or a double-headsail yawl. At the Boston show we went on an Orion 27, also built by Pacific Seacraft. Joyce liked the boat a lot and said so. I said, "If you like this boat you should see the Crealock 37, which I saw at the Annapolis show". Mary Cady, the dealer, heard us and said that their own Crealock 37 was at a boatyard in Portsmouth, New Hampshire and she would call us when they took the cover off if we would like to see it. We said we would and gave her our telephone number.

In April Mary Cady called and said they had taken the cover off their boat and we made arrangements to go see it the next Saturday. We spent several hours exploring the boat and talking with Mary and Roger Cady. We discussed various options, upholstery, and many other details. At that time there was no other Crealock 37 in New England and they were anxious to sell one. As a result they offered us a substantial discount from the list price. We said we would consider it and let them know. On the way home we talked about the possibility of buying a Crealock 37. We also talked about our dearest friends, Ranger and Helena Farrell, who were our age. Ranger was partially paralyzed and couldn't talk because of a stroke, and Helena had died from breast cancer. My conclusion was, "What are we waiting for? We don't know how much time we have left. Let's do it!" Joyce concurred. On Monday I called the Cadys and told them our decision. They said they would place the order and later called us back to say our boat should be ready some time in June.

We put *Pearl II* on the market and hired a broker. He called after about a week and said he had a couple who wanted to see the boat on Saturday, but he was not available and could I show it. I did. Monday he called with an offer. It was much too low and I made a counter offer. After this I had many telephone conversations with the broker about the price the buyer was willing to pay, and finally agreed on a price well below my asking price. I later came across the buyer at Logan airport and he told me he had been willing to pay my asking price. I had thought a broker worked for the seller. This broker had not even seen *Pearl II* and was in no position to determine what a fair price would be.

The new boat was to be named *Pearl III*. In the spring I went to Los Angeles on a business trip and had the opportunity to visit the Pacific Seacraft factory in Fullerton and see *Pearl III* under construction.

Pearl III under Construction

On June 20th Mary Cady called and said the boat would be shipped the next day and should arrive in about a week. On the 29th she called and said *Pearl III* was in Connecticut and should arrive at Barden's Boatyard in a few hours. We drove to Marion to be there for the arrival and were excited when the truck drove in to Barden's Boat yard. The boat was beautiful and

Pearl III Arrives at Barden's Boat Yard

we couldn't wait to get it in the water! Mary Cady was there, and Roger Cady was there to rig the boat after it was launched. We found out later that a bridge in Connecticut had collapsed just before *Pearl III* got there and the truck had to detour around it. We came close to losing *Pearl III* before we even got her!

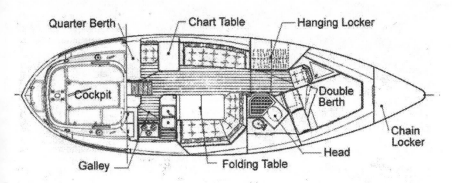

Pearl III Layout

In the forward cabin there is a diagonal double berth, a hanging locker, an upholstered seat, and many drawers and lockers.

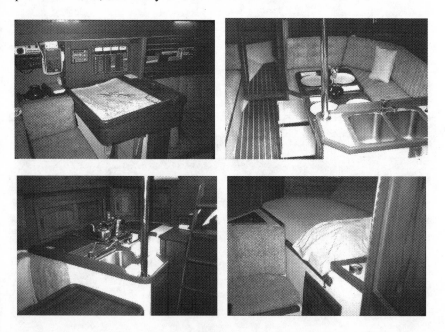

Pearl III Interior

On the starboard side across from the hanging locker is an enclosed compartment with a marine head and sink. There is a teak grating on the floor and a shower drain under it.

On the port side of the main cabin are a settee-berth, a chart table and seat, and a large quarter berth. On the starboard side is an L-shaped seat wrapping around two sides of a folding table. Aft of this is a galley with a double sink, 3-burner stove and oven, and a large icebox. There is a filler to make the L-shaped seat into a double berth when the table is folded.

Pearl III Sail Plan and Underbody

Pearl III is a double-headsail yawl. The jib (yankee) is roller furling on aluminum extrusions. The stays'l is roller furling on a wire. This turned out to be a good choice. When we later bought a genoa jib we found it difficult to tack it around the rolled-up stays'l, so we would lower the stays'l partway and lash it to the bottom of the mast in an "L" shape. The small mizzen was not as effective as the one on *Pearl II* in keeping the bow from falling off when anchoring or picking up a mooring, but it was better than a sloop. In heavy weather the boat was well balanced under the mizzen and stays'l. The five sails provided a lot of sail options for various wind conditions, but we did miss the self-tacking jib that we had on *Pearl II*. To make sail handling easier *Pearl III* had a single-handlers package so all halyards and furling lines were led back to the cockpit.

The Crealock 37 has a split underbody with a fairly long keel and a rudder on a skeg, with a bridge between the keel and the skeg. It is not as good with lobster pot buoys and warps in Maine waters as the full-keel Cape Dory, but it is better than a fin-keel boat with an exposed propeller. Under sail a pot warp can be caught on the skeg after passing under the keel. When this happens under power the warp is close to the propeller and easily can be sucked in.

We had purchased a loran for *Pearl II* in 1981 when lat-long conversion became available. Roger installed the antenna on *Pearl III's* mizzenmast before the boat was launched. *Pearl III* also had a bulkhead-mounted compass, a knotlog, a Signet depthsounder, a wind meter, and a radiotelephone.

Power is a four-cylinder 32-horsepower Universal diesel engine, with a 40-gallon diesel tank under the cabin sole. There are water tanks under the forward berth and the quarter berth, holding a total of 85 gallons. The water system is pressurized and running the engine provides hot water.

I had read that the boat was so well-balanced under sail that a wheel was not necessary – it easily could be handled with a tiller. So we ordered it with a tiller, which provides more room in the cockpit. We also ordered a teak cockpit grating and a below decks autopilot. With the autopilot in use the tiller can be raised and the cockpit is unencumbered.

Pearl III had two bow rollers and we kept two anchors on them. One was a 35 lb. CQR and the other was a 22 lb. Bruce. Each one had 25 ft. of chain and a 150 ft. nylon rode. The rodes were shackled together at the bitter ends, so we could deploy 300 ft. of rode on either of the anchors. In addition we had a 27 lb. high-tensile aluminum Fortress anchor as a storm anchor. The anchor could be disassembled for storage and we kept it under the port settee berth. Although light in weight it had the holding power of a 50 lb. Danforth anchor

We had shakedown cruises every weekend during July, visiting Hadley Harbor, Tarpaulin Cove, and Redbrook Harbor. During our cruise to Redbrook Harbor we discovered the "Chart Room", a restaurant at King's Marina. The Chartroom is housed in a converted railroad barge, which gives it a unique atmosphere. It also has an addition on the waterside that provides a panoramic view of the harbor. The Chart Room always was crowded with boaters and motorists when we went there. The food and drinks were excellent and a special attraction to boaters was that you could tie up at their floats and walk directly in to the restaurant. Redbrook Harbor was one of our favorite weekend cruises for many years and we frequently tied up at the float at noontime and went to the Chartroom for bloody marys and stuffed Quahogs.

Autopilot in Use and Joyce Enjoying the Ride

15

TO MAINE ON *PEARL III*, etc.

By the end of July we were anxious to get to Maine. We left Marion on Sunday July 31st on a three-week cruise. The boys were now old enough to have activities of their own, so it was just the two of us. Our first stop was Provincetown, where we anchored in the harbor at 8:55 PM and had dinner. Winds gusting to 40 knots were forecast so it was a good chance to test the Bruce anchor, which we had been using as our working anchor although it weighed only 22 lbs. I put out the two anchors with the rode of the CQR left slack so the load would be on the Bruce. The rode of the CQR was still slack in the morning, indicating that the Bruce had held.

August 2nd we weighed anchor at 8:00 AM and were at the Race Point bell at 10:10. Our destination from there was Matinicus Rock, a distance of 121 nautical miles. The day was overcast with a southwest wind of 10 to 12 knots and we used our working sails. Around noon we sighted several whales and a ship headed for Boston. At 5:30 PM the wind died and we turned on the engine. From then on the wind was variable and we alternated between motoring and sailing. The next morning it was sunny and at nine Matinicus Rock was on the port beam. We changed course, heading for our favorite spot, McGlathery Island, where we anchored at 4:45 PM.

Pearl III Anchored at McGlathery Island in Favorite Spot

The windjammer *Heritage* was anchored in the cove and the crew and passengers went ashore and had a clambake on the beach. We were pleased to see that they were quiet and well-behaved, and that they cleaned up the beach when they were finished and left it just the way they had found it.

Windjammer *Heritage* Anchored at McGlathery Island

Thursday was a nice sunny day at McGlathery. I dug clams for chowder again. During the day *Heritage* left and two other windjammers came in and anchored. In addition, eight other sailboats came in for the night – the largest number we had ever seen there. I guess the word was spreading that it was a nice place to anchor. We were lucky to have arrived the previous day so we could anchor in our favorite spot near the rocky point on the north side of the cove.

Friday morning we headed for Northeast Harbor. We arrived in dense fog at 4:00 PM and picked up a rental mooring. There was fog off and on for two days. We went ashore and got provisions and left our laundry at "The Shirt of your Back". Saturday evening we had dinner at a new restaurant, "The Popplestone".

We got water and ice the next morning and left Northeast Harbor at 8:45 heading east and passed the Schoodic bell in a north wind of 10 to 15 knots. We crossed Petit Manan bar at 12:33 PM after an hour of motoring because the wind had died. We dropped our anchor in the Cows Yard between Head Harbor Island and Steele Harbor Island at 5:00 PM (see chart on page 145). It had been a nice sunny day, but most of the day was windless.

In the morning the fog was thick and we hung around the Cows Yard all day. This appeared to be a beautiful well-protected harbor, but we didn't see much of it because of the fog. From there we motored in the fog to Lakeman Harbor, near Roque Island (see chart on page 49). We anchored in 13 feet of water close up to a cliff on Marsh Island. I climbed the cliff and took pictures of *Pearl III* from the top.

Pearl III at Lakeman Harbor

The chart showed a depth of two feet at low water so we didn't plan to stay there overnight. After lunch the fog cleared and we motored over to the Roque Island beach, anchored, and went ashore. The dinghy almost swamped landing in the waves crashing on the beach. After landing we climbed the steps leading to the top and looked out over the beach. We spent the night anchored in Bunker Cove and weighed anchor at 9:20 in the morning heading west. The weather was sunny and clear and the wind was northwest at 5 to 10 knots. During the day it varied between five and 15 knots.

We sailed to Inner Winter Harbor and picked up the mooring of a lobster boat that had been hauled for repairs. Over the years we found the lobstermen at Winter Harbor to be very friendly, always pointing out a mooring that we could use for the night. We had dinner at Chase's. The night was beautiful and calm. The 50-gallon water tank ran out. It had lasted for four days and two showers.

We left Winter Harbor heading west with a light and variable wind and went through Casco Passage and York Narrows, planning to try Eggemoggin Reach for the first time. It turned out to be not much of a reach for us because there was no wind. After motoring through the reach we anchored in Bucks Harbor. A few minutes after our arrival a couple rowed up and said they were the O'Brions and were interested in the Crealock 37. The Cadys knew we were in Maine and had told them to watch for our boat. Shortly after that the *Bearings* (the Cady's Boat) arrived with two couples on charter. They were to meet the Cadys in Camden at noon on Monday, four days later.

It rained steadily all night and all the next day so we stayed put in Bucks Harbor. The dinghy was full of water, with the oars floating. I bailed it using a small electric bilge pump that I had bought for the purpose (I also had installed 12 volt outlets outside, one in the cockpit, and one forward to plug in a searchlight..

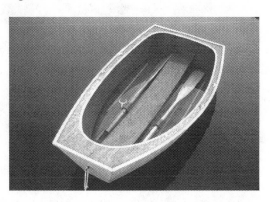

Oars Floating in the Dinghy

Saturday was clear, cold, and sunny with a north wind at 10 to 20 knots. We sailed out of Bucks Harbor and Eggemoggin Reach, then tacked north to Castine and picked up Eaton's Boat Yard's guest mooring. We rowed ashore and walked up the hill to Fort George, where there was a bicentennial celebration of the Castine/St. Andrews connection underway. During the Revolutionary War the people in Castine were loyal to the Crown and were expelled from Castine. They packed up their belongings and resettled in St. Andrews, New Brunswick. Some of the houses were floated to St. Andrews on barges.

Eaton's Boat Yard, Castine

Castine/St. Andrews Bicentennial Celebration

We got provisions including two 10-pound blocks of ice and a bag of cubes, went to the local museum, and had an excellent dinner at Rafferty's Restaurant.

Castine was an interesting town on a steep hill rising up from the waterfront. It also was the home of the Maine Marine Maritime Academy, with a large ship, the *State of Maine*, docked at the waterfront.

Castine Main Street

State of Maine

Sunday morning was sunny and the wind was from the southwest at 10 to 15 knots. We tacked down East Penobscot Bay against the wind and with an ebbing current. After an hour of slow progress we started motor sailing. At 6:10 PM we picked up a mooring in the Camden outer harbor. In the morning we motored in to Willey Wharf for water, ice and CNG. The deck fill covers were not well marked and a few minutes after I started filling what I thought was the water tank some brown liquid bubbled out. I had filled the diesel tank with water – about 20 gallons! The Willey people pumped it out and thought they had it all. Then they added four cans of "Heet" to absorb the water, and filled the tank with diesel. The Cadys arrived in *Bearings* while this was going on and we agreed to meet at Tenants Harbor in the evening.

We left Willey Wharf at 1:45 PM and at 2:45 the engine quit. The Racor filter was full of water. Because of limited knowledge I didn't want to mess around so we drifted back to the Camden outer harbor in light wind and picked up a mooring. In the morning I rowed in to Wayfarer Marine and they towed *Pearl III* in to their dock. At 8:30 Edwin Lord came aboard and worked on the engine. He bled the fuel lines, changed the filters, and changed the oil. He recommended that we run the tank almost dry before adding fuel and that we drain the tank for the winter.

At 1:00 PM we left Wayfarer Marine under power heading for Tenants Harbor. The wind was from the southwest and varied from 5 to 20 knots, so we sailed and motor-sailed to Tenants Harbor, arriving at 8:00 PM. In the morning, Wednesday August 15th, we went ashore for provisions, including fresh haddock from Cod End. We weighed anchor at about noon and sailed to Cranberry Island, just south of Friendship in Muscongus Bay, with a cold southwest wind of 15 knots. We anchored on the north side of Cranberry Island at 5:00 PM.

Thursday morning we left Cranberry Island at ten, motoring and sailing off and on in a light southwest wind and light fog, past Pemaquid Point, the Cuckolds, and Fuller Rock. We anchored at Jewel Island at 5:15 PM.

Pearl III at Jewel Island

We weighed anchor in the morning at 8:11 on Friday August 18th. The next stop was to be Marion. It was hazy with light fog and a west wind of 8 to 10 knots. The first leg of the trip would be to the Race Point bell. We sailed down the west side of Jewel Island, past Inner Green Island, and at Outer Green Island set a course of 200 degrees magnetic for the Race Point buoy at a distance of 95 nautical miles. During the day the fog burned off and it became nice and sunny. The wind varied from west to southwest at 8 to 15 knots. At 3:15 PM we sighted two whales on the starboard side – at 3:45 more whales on the same side doing gymnastics. At 5:00 there were

The only Whale Photo We Could Get

more whales. Unfortunately none of them were within good camera range. At 11:45 PM the wind died and we started the engine. From there to the canal the engine was off and on depending on the wind.

At 5:25 the next morning there were two whales near the boat on the starboard side. At 6:35 the Provincetown Monument* was visible and in a short time we were at the Race Point bell. We tacked and motor-sailed across Cape Cod Bay and entered the canal at 2:00 PM. The current turned against us at 2:20 so it was a slow passage. The sail to Marion in Buzzards Bay was wild. The wind was west with gusts over 30 knots. We finally picked up our mooring in Marion at 5:30 PM. Our elapsed time from Jewel Island was 33-1/2 hours. A long poke except for Buzzards Bay!

The Provincetown Monument

The next morning Joyce drove Tim several miles to Denny's, where he worked. The dinghy was still on the roof of the car. When she came back she announced that the dinghy had blown off the roof and gone bow-first into a utility pole. Then I remembered – I had untied it the night before, but I was tired and left it on the roof to be taken off in the morning. – then forgot all about it. I drove out and brought it home; it was a total loss and we needed a new dinghy. I had seen what looked like the perfect dinghy to go with *Pearl III*. Designed by Robert Perry it was a double-ender like *Pearl III*. It had teak floorboards, teak gratings on the seats, and was

---

*The Provincetown Monument is the tallest granite structure in the United States at 252 feet. It was dedicated in 1910 to commemorate the first landing of the Pilgrims at Provincetown in 1620.

called a "Perrywinkle" after its designer. It looked like the ultimate dinghy. We ordered one and had it shipped from the west coast in time for the next boating season

The winter Cover

In the fall of 1983 I made a wood frame and covered *Pearl III* with plastic tarps. The ridgepole was 2 x 4's. The side pieces were 1 x 3 strapping with wood blocks screwed to them. The blocks had holes that fit down over the tops of the stanchions. The "rafters " were 1 x 3 strapping hinged together at the ridge. The whole thing was screwed together. I used this frame for 22 years with only minor repairs: some of the screws had to be moved because the holes wore out, and two of the rafters broke from snow loads and had to be replaced. The plastic tarps had to be replaced every three or four years, but this was much less expensive and more environmentally friendly than shrink-wrap, which was the popular method of covering in the 90's and had to be discarded each year.

During the winter I purchased a "cruising shooter". This was a downwind sail that was a cross between a spinnaker and a genoa jib. It was made of nylon and, like a spinnaker, was not hanked to the forestay.

Our trouble with water in the diesel tank was not yet over. The Heet that Willey Wharf had put in the diesel tank to absorb water attacked the plastic bowl on the Racor filter and it had to be replaced. Another related problem was caused by the fact that the engine sump held 11 quarts of oil. Mr. Lord didn't know this (most sumps hold only four or five quarts) and as a result at least four quarts of oil ended up in the bilge and it took years to get it all cleaned out. This large sump capacity also made changing the oil very difficult and time consuming.

1984 was not a good year for sailing. Joyce went to Bermuda with my sister, we went to California to visit our son John and his wife and daughter, we spent a week at Star Island at a family conference, and we went to Phoenix, Arizona where I accepted an award from the American Institute of Architects on behalf of Bolt Beranek and Newman. So our only boating activities were local weekend cruises, and a cruise to Provincetown.

One weekend we went to dinner at a nice restaurant, "Le Grenier" at Vineyard Haven. We asked for two glasses of wine and the waiter said, "I'm sorry, we don't serve wine. You have to bring your own bottle." There were four people at the next table, obviously from a boat. They overheard our conversation with the waiter and one of them turned to us and said they had more wine than they wanted and we could have either white or red. Then he passed us a bottle of Chardonnay.

In August Earle Koile, an old friend from our Burlington, Vermont days, called from Texas and said that he would be attending a conference in Provincetown and that he and his wife Carmon were driving up from Austin. I said Joyce and I would sail to Provincetown to see them, and if the weather was good we could all go for a sail. The weather was good the day we sailed out and also the next day. We drove around town in their new Mercedes and went for a sail in the afternoon, and then went out to dinner. It was a pleasant reunion.

Carmon and Earle Koile, and Joyce   Dick and Jackie Stone

Late in the season we sailed to Hadley Harbor with our next door neighbors, Dick and Jackie Stone. Dick and Don Sullivan had sold the *Scrimshaw* and the Stones were boatless. Don bought another boat, but for some reason unknown to me, Dick, who was an avid sailor, never did. We poked into Wild Harbor but didn't stay – it was full of rocks and open to the southwest wind. The weather was chilly but it was sunny and there were nice winds, so we had a pleasant time.

When we first went to Hadley Harbor there were only a few moorings and there always was plenty of space for anchoring. But the owners of Naushon Island put in more and more moorings so that eventually there was no space for anchoring. Unoccupied moorings were available for visiting yachtsmen and when the moorings were all taken it was possible to anchor in the outer harbor, which was not as snug as the inner harbor.

16

PACIFIC SEACRAFT RENDEZVOUS AND MAINE

In August 1985 Pacific Seacraft held a rendezvous at Block Island. Joyce and I thought it would be fun to see other Pacific Seacraft boats and meet their owners so we decide to attend. Our visit to the rendezvous was to be the first part of a four-week cruise that would include about three weeks in Maine. We left Marion at 2:00 PM on Friday the 2nd of August. The wind was northeast at 10 knots, much better than the prevailing southwest wind for sailing down the bay. Our intention was to sail to Cuttyhunk, pick up a mooring, stay there for the night, and then go on to Block Island the next day. When we got to Cuttyhunk at 6:00 PM the pond and outer harbor were packed with boats and no moorings were available, so we left the harbor and continued on to Block Island. It was a beautiful moonlit night and the wind continued from the northeast at 10 to 15 knots. We alternated on two-hour watches during the night and arrived at Block Island and anchored in the Great Salt Pond at 2:00 PM the next day. On our way to the anchorage we passed many Pacific Seacraft boats: Flickas, Orions, and two Crealock 37's.

The Great Salt Pond at Block Island

We had a short nap and brunch and called for the launch. There were only two launches serving this huge anchorage and it took an hour for it to arrive. We checked in at rendezvous headquarters, bought clambake tickets, and were given a small engraved plaque to put on our bulkhead. There were various activities over the weekend: a tug-of-war, a water-balloon fight, and a sailboat race. After registering we went to Sam Peckham's Tavern where the clambake would be held and had two gin and tonics. There was a good guitar-playing folk singer who sang an interesting song entitled "Marbles". At the clambake we talked with Pacific Seacraft's interior designer and told him we thought he had done a nice job on the Crealock 37. We also talked with Mike Howarth, the plant manager and one of Pacific Seacraft's owners, and invited him to visit *Pearl III* in the morning. We had another long wait for the launch to go back to the boat and toured the entire harbor before being dropped off.

Mike Howarth came aboard Sunday morning and we had a nice chat. He thought the boat looked great and said they couldn't get teak that was as nice as ours anymore. He asked about problems and we told him that the head sink faucet didn't work very well and that the head filled up with water. He said they had changed to a bronze faucet (ours was plastic) and that he would send us one and a valve to put on the head water intake hose. There was a race later in the morning and we were leading the fleet until we looked back and saw all the boats turning around, so we did too. It turned out that the course had been shortened and it was announced by VHF. We didn't have the announcement channel and missed the announcement. Otherwise we would have won the race. Apparently our mizzen made us a little faster than the Crealock 37 sloops.

A few notes on Block Island: the marinas are full of big ugly powerboats with plastic furniture; the waterfront is unattractive with slummy buildings; and Sam Peckham's clambake was so-so, with good chowder, corn, and sausages, but mediocre lobsters.

From Block Island we sailed back to Cuttyhunk. The weather was perfect with a southwest wind of 10 to 20 knots. We sailed with the main and cruising shooter all the way and picked up a mooring in the outer harbor. at Cuttyhunk. Just after we poured our before-dinner drinks the "Harbor Raw Bar" arrived and we bought a dozen shrimp to go with the drinks.

We left Cuttyhunk at 8:00 AM and sailed to Padanarum under main and cruising shooter. It took a while to learn how to get the cruising shooter up and down but I finally got it. We got fuel, ice, water, and also bought a pair of seven-foot oars. Our beautiful Shaw and Tenney spruce oars with leathers had been stolen from our driveway. We thought Concordia Yachts would have good oars, but the ones they had were thick ash and very heavy. We needed oars so we were stuck with them. At the end of the cruise I spent a lot of time planing them down to a reasonable thickness.

The Cruising Shooter

From Padanarum we sailed to Bassetts Island, near the west end of the Cape Cod Canal, and anchored in the cove on the north side of the island. The Perrywinkle was heavier and wider than our previous dinghies and I spent a long time hoisting it and lashing it down on deck; we never towed a dinghy offshore after loosing *Nit 1* while towing it in a storm. At 7:15 PM we left Bassetts Island and motored through the canal to the Harbor of Refuge at the east end of the canal. There was no wind and I spent most of the night fending off boats that were drifting around in all directions.

We go up at 6:15, had breakfast, and headed for the Race Point bell. There was no wind and the motor was on all the way to the bell. It was a beautiful sunny day and whale-watching boats were dashing out from Provincetown loaded with pilgrims hoping to see some "spouters". At the bell I put up the main, mizzen, and cruising shooter. We drifted along at about four knots. We planned to go farther east than we had in the past, so we were headed for Mt. Desert Rock. It was a bright and sunny day; the wind was off and on and so was the motor. At 4:00 PM the wind picked up from the south-southeast and we were moving along at 6-1/2 knots. During the night we sailed most of the time, motoring only about three hours. At 7:00 it was bright and clear with a southwest wind of 10 knots and we were sailing along wing-and-wing with the main, mizzen, and cruising shooter.

The wind died the next morning and we spent the rest of the day motoring off and on. At 10:15 AM we were 19 miles from Mt. Desert Rock and changed our course to the gong at Western Way and the entrance to Northeast Harbor. At 5:30 PM we picked up a mooring in Northeast Harbor. Our log indicated that we had come 182 miles from the Harbor of Refuge. It had taken 35 hours, so our average speed was 5.2 knots. We went ashore for ice and then had dinner aboard.

Wing-and-Wing with Perrywinkle on Deck

Thursday morning August 8th we went ashore, went to the hardware store and the Pine Tree Market, had a lunch of seafood chowder and lobster rolls at Docksider's, and bought ice cream cones. On the way back to *Pearl III* we spotted *Pearl II* in the harbor and rowed over. Mike and Sherry Missig, the new owners, invited us aboard. The boat looked good, but they apologized for the exterior teak (which wasn't bad). They had put a fire in the Cole stove the night before and enjoyed it a lot. We decided we must get a cabin heater for next year.

Another surprise in Northeast Harbor was to see Ira and Betty Dyer rowing by on their way ashore. Ira was a colleague of mine at Bolt Beranek and Newman. I hailed them and invited them to come aboard on their way back, which they did. They were on a Blue Water Cruise. After a nice visit with them I called the Asticou Inn where we hoped to go for dinner, but their Thursday evening buffet was very popular and they were all booked up. Instead we had a good dinner at the Popplestone. In all our visits to Northeast Harbor we never did get to have dinner at the Asticou.

Friday was a nice sunny say. We left Northeast Harbor heading east under power and turned the engine off just before Tit Manan when the wind reached 10 knots from the southwest. We passed Great Wass Island, turned on the engine, and motored up the Mudhole Channel to the Mudhole.

The Asticou Inn at Northeast Harbor

At low tide the entrance is blocked by ledges and it is not possible to get in or out. It was well after low tide when we arrived at the entrance so we had no problem getting in. There were no other boats and we dropped the anchor in 25' of water, rowed ashore to the west end of the harbor, and walked south on a dirt road. A short distance along the road there was a small pond with several dozen ducks that came right over to see us. There was a sign on the road that said "Duck Crossing". When we got back to the boat we grilled excellent steaks from the Pine Tree market on the charcoal grille.

Calm Water in the Mudhole

Going Ashore at the Mudhole

Saturday morning when we motored out of the Mudhole we picked up a large clump of seaweed on the propeller. I was able to hook it off with the

Libby Islands Light*

boathook, standing on my head over the side with Joyce holding on to my feet. There was a light breeze and we motor-sailed east past the Libby Islands to Cutler. Just before we turned in to Cutler harbor we could see the cliffs of Grand Manan Island and the coast of Nova Scotia 40 miles away. Cutler is a pretty little harbor and is the jumping off point for many boats cruising to Nova Scotia. After anchoring in the harbor we rowed ashore and bought lobsters at Corbett's Wharf, which was a short walk away from the dock.

Cutler Harbor

*There is a sand bar between the two Libby Islands that is covered at high tide, and before the lighthouse was built many ships came to grief passing through what was thought to be open water between the two islands. Old journals report 38 major wrecks around the Libby Islands in one 50 year period.

From Cutler we headed back west and had a nice sail to Roque Island. We anchored on the north side of the island in Shorey Cove, next to a cliff at the east end of the cove (see chart on page 49). We had a late lunch of balogna, cheese and lettuce sandwiches, and Knorr chicken-vegetable soup, then walked on the beach for a while. There were no other boats in the cove except for those of the owners at the other end of the beach. It was quite a fleet: a black schooner, a Friendship sloop, two lobster boats, a one-car ferry, and a seaplane!

We left Shorey Cove at 9:30 Monday morning in a 10 to 15 knot north wind. The sky was overcast but looked like clearing. The wind died half-way to Petit Manan but picked up later from the northwest at 15 to 20 knots and the sky cleared, so it was bright and sunny when we arrived at Inner Winter Harbor at 5:30 PM.

Pearl III at Shorey Cove   Dinghy and Friends–Winter Harbor

As usual a lobsterman pointed to an empty mooring saying, "Take that one, the boat's been hauled". We rowed ashore and walked up the hill to Chase's, where we had a good shore dinner.

We had made arrangements to meet Stan and Cindy Hamlet at Rockport on Thursday. Stan and Cindy, who now lived in Vermont, were former neighbors of ours in Lexington before we built the Baskin Road house. I called the "Sail Loft" restaurant in Rockport and made reservations for four at 8:00 PM on Thursday.

In the morning I got two blocks of ice and two bags of cubes before we left Winter Harbor at nine bound for McGlathery Island. It was a beautiful sunny day with a blue sky, white clouds, and a light west wind – not the best wind for the way we were going. We arrived at McGlathery in the afternoon, rowed ashore and walked on the rocks. We never tired of this beautiful island with its fir trees, granite rocks and outcroppings

Relaxing in the Cockpit at McGlathery Island

After a quiet night we left at 9:30 in the morning. The sea was calm and the wind was light so we motored most of the way to Camden. After motoring around the outer harbor looking for a mooring we called Wayfarer Marine to find out if they had one available but got no answer. We finally found one on the north side of the outer harbor far from the town. We rowed a long distance to get ashore and had trouble finding a place to land the dinghy. We had to leave it at the town dock, which was very busy and not a good place to leave a dinghy, but we had no choice. The landing problem was created when a large part of the shoreline on the town side of the harbor was developed into condominiums (or apartments) with use of the docks limited to the occupants.

Camden Harbor Condominiums

We bought crabmeat sandwiches and fruit juice drinks for lunch and then bought groceries and steak at a local market. The streets were bumper to bumper with tourists. The next morning Joyce took the laundry ashore and I took the boat to Willey Wharf for diesel, water, ice, and CNG. They were out of CNG. When we bought *Pearl III,* CNG looked like the boat-stove fuel of the future. Unlike propane it is lighter than air and if there is a leak it will not end up in the bilge, where it could explode. This advantage apparently did not compensate for the lightweight tanks of propane and its widespread availability. (CNG tanks must withstand pressures in excess of 2,000 psi and are very heavy.) Propane became the stove fuel of choice and all new boats came with propane stoves. The only other places CNG was available down east were Boothbay and Southwest Harbor.

The trip to Rockport, where we were to meet the Hamlets, was only 6-1/2 miles. We motored to the Rockport Marine dock at the head of the harbor and were assigned a mooring. From the mooring we rowed ashore and trudged up a steep hill to the grocery store and bought supplies and Popsicles, then rowed back to the boat. Then we donned our fancy duds and rowed ashore to meet the Hamlets. The Sail Loft hostess had no record of our reservation, but the Hamlets had been in at 5:00 PM and made reservations for four. They arrived a short time later and treated us to a delicious seafood dinner. When we left the Sail Loft the sky opened up with a downpour, thunder, and lightening. After it stopped I rowed out and took *Pearl III* in to the dock and we loaded the Hamlet's gear.

We left Rockport in the morning and sailed across West Penobscot Bay to Pulpit Harbor, where we anchored and rowed to the dock at the end of the harbor. Looking at the photo with three people in the dinghy, I don't see how another person was able to fit in. Somehow four of us did fit in,

Cindy, Me, and Stan in the Perrywinkle

rowed ashore, and started walking to North Haven 4-1/2 miles away. As we were walking a blue pickup truck stopped and gave us a lift almost into town. We bought film, ice cream cones, and postcards, which we wrote and mailed. On the way back to Pulpit Harbor the same truck picked us up and took us almost all the way to the harbor. Back aboard *Pearl III* we had drinks and then a good steak for dinner. The rest of the evening we spent talking and watching windjammers and other boats sailing into the harbor.

Spinnakers Flying

Saturday morning August 17th we sailed/motored to Carvers Harbor at Vinalhaven. It was a sunny blue-sky day with fluffy white clouds. On the way to Carvers Harbor there was a sailboat race on the downwind leg with spinnakers flying. A beautiful sight on a beautiful day.

Going in to Carvers Harbor we stopped and bought lobsters, then anchored in an open space in the northeast corner of the harbor. After anchoring we went ashore, walked around town, and bought ice cream cones. (It seems that we were buying ice cream cones everywhere we went.) After the walk it was back to *Pearl III* for a lobster dinner.

Pearl III at Rockport   Cindy and Stan

The following morning I had trouble raising the anchor. Stan and I both pulled on the rode and gradually got it up far enough to see that the anchor was hooked on a heavy chain, probably from an old mooring. After a struggle we finally got it unhooked, got the mud off, and were on our way back to Rockport to drop off Cindy and Stan. There was no wind and we motored up the coast of Vinalhaven almost to Fox Islands Thorofare, where the wind picked up and we were able to sail across West Penobscot Bay to Rockport. It was another nice sunny day. After dropping off Cindy and Stan we headed east and sailed to Tenants Harbor, where we picked up a rental mooring.

Monday morning August 19th was cloudy and hazy, and rain was forecast. We went ashore and got food and ice from the market up the hill,and a nice piece of sole and some charts from Cod End. While there I told Mrs. Miller that the first time I had been there the fish was kept in a large walk-in cooler. She said it had been cooled by 500-pound blocks of ice. They were delivered by truck and slid down a ramp into the store. One day a block got loose at the top of the ramp, gained speed down the ramp, and shot through the entire length of the store, smashed through the door at the other end, and came to rest out on the dock! Luckily no one was in the way. Since that time Cod End had been modernized. Some of the fish was displayed behind glass under a counter like in a supermarket. The rest of it was stored in a large modern refrigerator

After getting back to the boat we just hung around until 2:40 PM and then left for Maplejuice Cove, up the St. George River. The wind was northeast at 8 to 10 knots and it was rainy and foggy. Right after we left Tenants Harbor something happened to Joyce's back and she stayed in the cabin on the port berth all the way, in terrible pain. Instead of Maplejuice Cove I dropped anchor on the east side of the river in Turkey Cove, which had better protection from the easterly wind. It was rainy and windy all night.

Maplejuice Cove

The morning was peaceful. The wind was gone and the clouds were breaking up, but Joyce's back was no better. The sun broke out about noon and we motored across the river to Maplejuice Cove. It is a large, pretty cove on the west side of the river and reminded me of the LaHave River. Seven cruising sailboats arrived in the evening, including *Spring Moon*, a Crealock 37. Joyce's back was bad. She could hardly move and needed medical attention. I knew there was a hospital at Boothbay, so we would go there in the morning.

Wednesday was a nice day but there was no wind. After we had motored half way to Boothbay the wind came up from the southwest and we sailed the rest of the way to Boothbay and tied up at Brown's Wharf on the east side of the harbor. They called us a cab that took us to St. Andrew's Hospital on the other side of the harbor. When we got there I found out that the hospital had a dock, so I walked back to Brown's Wharf and brought *Pearl III* over and tied up at the hospital dock.

Pearl III at St. Andrews Hospital Dock

Dr. Andre Benoit had x-rays taken and said he thought Joyce had a compression fracture of the lower spine, but he was not a radiologist and couldn't be sure. He gave Joyce a prescription for a muscle relaxant and one for pain relief. We got the prescriptions filled and she got some sleep that night after taking them as directed. In the morning she could walk and felt 100% better. We got CNG and water at Pierce Marine. The price of the CNG was more than double the cost at Burr Brothers in Marion. I was surprised they didn't charge for the water! Next we tied up at the public float and took the Rocktide Inn Trolley to a shopping center outside town, where we had shrimp rolls for lunch and bought scotch, gin, and vermouth. (We really needed them after Joyce's back problem.) After taking the trolley back to town we bought some groceries and went back to the boat.

We left Boothbay at 1:30 PM on Thursday August 22nd. Our destination was Christmas Cove where we planned to have dinner at the Coveside Restaurant and spend the night. We picked up a mooring in Christmas Cove and had a wonderful haddock dinner at the Coveside Restaurant followed by Maine blueberry pie and ice cream. In the harbor we saw a Crealock 37 yawl just like ours nearby named *Isabelle*. It turned out that it was the Cady's boat renamed and now owned by Jack Schroeder, who lives year-round in Maine. *Isabelle* had a neat green dodger but didn't sit well on her lines; she was down in the stern and up in the bow. I had noticed the same thing with *Pearl III* shortly after she was put in the water at Barden's Boatyard and had put eight 25-pound lead bricks in the chain locker to get her to sit level in the water. The Crealock 37's probably were designed this way so that an all-chain rode would provide the weight required to level the boat in the water..

Friday morning was bright and sunny with white cumulous clouds, but very little wind. It was a perfect day to go to Monhegan Island, which was only 23 miles away. We left Christmas Cove about noon and motored most of the way to Monhegan. The Cruising Guide said the harbor was not a good place for a cruising sailboat to stay overnight. The moorings are for fishing boats and the bottom is full of old chains and other junk, so anchoring is not a good idea. We asked a fisherman if there was a mooring we could use for a few hours and he pointed one out. We rowed ashore and

Monhegan Harbor and Hotel

left the dinghy on a small beach with a lot of other dinghies and kids swimming, then walked up a dirt road to the Lighthouse and went to the museum. There were interesting exhibits about the island's flora and fauna and the history of the island. Upstairs there were paintings by some of the artists who had spent time on the island, including Rockwell Kent. Strangely there were none by Jamie Wyeth.

We left Monhegan at 4:00 PM and sailed to Burnt Island in a light south-west wind and anchored in the cove on the north side of the island. This is a nice anchorage when the weather is good and the wind is from the west or southwest. There is an abandoned Coast Guard station on the island that now seems to be used by fishermen. Dinner was chicken breasts and noodles cooked in white wine, broccoli, cookies, and milk.

The Cove at Burnt Island

After dinner I spent several hours in the dinghy unhooking the cruising shooter sheet from the propeller. The propeller can easily be seen from the dinghy, and it usually is possible to painstakingly untangle lines that are tangled around it using the extending boathook. The cruising shooter has turned out to be a difficult sail to use. When raising it the halyard often hooks on something near the top of the mast making it hard to get the head of the sail to the top of the mast, and there were other difficulties in flying it. When we got a roller-furling genoa jib the next year we stopped using the cruising shooter and used the genoa with a downwind pole instead.

The next day was Saturday. We left early and headed for that beautiful quiet anchorage in Quahog Bay, about 30 miles away. We went to the same location we had been to before on *Pearl II*, and anchored in the same place to the east of Snow Island. Although the location was the same the environment was entirely different. There were powerboats, speedboats pulling water-skiers, eight other sailboats, people shouting, tents all over the islands, and evidence everywhere of the grosser side of life afloat. On the bright side – we had motored all the way from Burnt Island so there was plenty of hot water. I took the opportunity to shower and shampoo my hair and felt like a new man. We had drinks in the cockpit, then dinner below. After dinner it was reading in bed, Tolkien's Lord of the Rings for me and one of Lynn and Larry Pardey's cruising books for Joyce.

We left Quahog Bay at 11:00 the next morning in the rain, heading for South Freeport where we planned to go shopping at L.L.Bean. After a quiet start the wind came up, gusting to 25 knots. I suited up in my foul weather gear and a sou'wester hat from Nova Scotia and braved the elements while Joyce lounged around the cabin reading and listening to Beethoven's seventh symphony. Joyce heated clam chowder for lunch and when I tried to spoon it into my mouth in the cockpit the wind blew it up my nose. We arrived at South Freeport at 2:45 PM and called South Freeport Marine and got a mooring for the night. We went ashore and found a telephone and a sign that said that L.L. Bean would send a van if you called them, so we called and they sent a van and took us to the store. South Freeport around L.L.Bean's is populated with every discount store known to man. At Bean's Joyce bought two skirts and I looked at a Hon folding bicycle that I thought would be a good thing to have on the boat. We went back to the harbor and had a fish dinner at the Haraseeket Lunch. For desert we tried their chocolate cream pie, which the Cruising Guide to the New England Coast said was the best on the coast. We considered it to be just OK.

Joyce Waiting for L.L.Bean Van   Rowing Folding Bike to *Pearl III*

The next day, Monday, there was rain, fog, and drizzle so we kept *Pearl III* on the mooring and went to L.L.Bean again. Joyce bought corduroy slacks and flannel pajamas for the winter and I bought a folding bicycle. Then we bought lobsters at a store on the dock and cooked them for dinner.

While we were on the dock buying lobsters I met a man named Tom Hagen who was sailing a 1931 wooden yawl by himself. He brought it out and rafted up with us and came aboard for a chat. He said he had an advertising/marketing business on Lewis Wharf in Boston but keeps his boat in South Freeport and works a lot by phone. Tom loaned us a favorite book of his, "Carter's Coast of New England". It is a fascinating story written by Robert Carter about a cruise along the New England coast from Boston to Bar Harbor, that he took with some friends in 1858. They visited many of the harbors we have visited. They did a lot of fishing, which was the major source of food during the cruise. The number and sizes of the fish and lobsters they caught were incredible. The most amazing catch was a halibut almost six feet long. (Our boys tried fishing several times – I think they caught a small mackerel once.) Robert Carter's crew stopped at Jewel Island and got butter, eggs, and milk from a farmhouse on the island, another example of the changes that have occurred along the coast in the last 150 years (see pictures on page 235). In the fall and winter I tried to contact Tom to return the book, but there was no Tom Hagen at Lewis Wharf and I was never able to find him. Then I loaned the book to a friend and haven't yet gotten it back.

The next day I rowed my new bike ashore and peddled to a small store to buy eggs, milk, and a few other items. After trying the bike out I went back to L.L.Bean and bought one for Joyce, then we left South Freeport and motored and sailed to Jewel Island, only 10 miles away. We anchored in the cove and went ashore for a short walk. There were seven other sailboats in the cove and two other couples and a dog walking around, but there were no tents or other activity, probably because of the rainy weather for the past two days. The sun was now out and it was a beautiful afternoon. We had an early dinner of spaghetti and salad with red wine. Following dinner I hoisted the dinghy onto the cabin top and lashed it down in preparation for a trip to the Isles of Shoals the next day.

We left Jewel Island at 6:30 AM with a west wind at 10 to 12 knots and picked up a mooring in Gosport Harbor at 5:30 PM (See charts on pages 219 and 170). When we first went to Gosport Harbor with the Alacrity there were almost no moorings there except for a few belonging to fishermen on the northeast side of the harbor away from the hotel, but now the harbor was crowded with private moorings issued by the harbormaster in Rye, New Hampshire. We didn't go ashore because of the nuisance of unlashing the dinghy, hoisting it down, and then reversing the process later.

Something in the rigging was clunking around all night and we had a fitful sleep, got up early, and left the mooring before dawn headed for Provincetown. The wind was north at 10 to 12 knots and we moved along nicely with main, mizzen, and cruising shooter. After Cape Ann the wind died. At this point we thought about going straight to the canal instead of stopping at Provincetown. This would save a lot of time, so we turned on the engine and changed course to the canal. About this time a large infestation of flies came aboard and we were busy with two fly swatters for the rest of the afternoon. I lost count after we had swatted about a hundred of them, and they still kept coming. Where **do** they come from so far from land?

We arrived at the Harbor of Refuge at the east end of the Cape Cod Canal at 7:15 PM and anchored in the northeast corner near the fishing boats where there was good swinging room. Food was running low and we fell back on Dinty Moore's beef stew and red wine, the last of the wine. While we there we watched tuna being unloaded from a fishing boat.

Unloading Tuna at the Harbor of Refuge

We got an early start in the morning because the current would turn against us at 10:30. The weather was overcast and after we passed the Railroad Bridge it started to rain and blow, so we got into our foul-weather gear, which leaked at the seams in spite of its high cost. At the end of the canal it was raining and "blowing like stink", but we sailed along reasonably comfortably under yankee and mizzen. When we turned in towards Marion there was a sailboat motoring nearby and when we got to can "5" they began to crowd us. A little later at the nun they almost ran into us. I shouted out loudly, "Read the Rules of the Road! A sailing vessel has the right-of-way over a motoring vessel". Only then did they slow down and give way. We picked up our mooring at 1:30 PM in a big storm – rain, thunder, and lightning. Finally at 6:55 it calmed down enough so that we could motor in to the dock and tie up to go ashore for a bite to eat. When we came back there was another boat rafted up to *Pearl III* and the skipper was filling his water tanks. He asked if we were the ones that had tied up to his boat before and that when the tide had come up it ripped out his cleats. He made a few other choice remarks although his wife tried to shut him up. When he got his water tanks full and left the dock he almost rammed us in the starboard side. We guessed that he was drunk.

We stayed on the boat for the night and drove home in the morning. It was a good cruise except for the few unpleasant events on the last day, which was August 30th. We had been gone since the 2nd of the month. At four weeks this was our longest cruise and we had gone farther east on the Maine coast than we had gone before.

We Shared the Cape Cod Canal with Other Small Boats

17
HURRICANE GLORIA

In September 1985 hurricane Gloria hit Marion Harbor with a vengeance. I had gone down to Marion the day before and taken off the sails and almost everything else above deck that I could. The day after Gloria hit I drove down to Marion with fear and trepidation. When I looked out over the harbor my fear increased. The opposite shore and the marsh at the end of the harbor were littered with boats, but I couldn't see *Pearl III* anywhere.

Marion Harbor Shoreline the Day after Hurricane Gloria

I talked with one of Barden's workers and asked him if he knew where my boat was. He pointed across the harbor up towards the marsh at the end of the harbor and said she had dragged her mooring and was in shallow water, still attached to the mooring pennant and anchor. It was then low tide and after he pointed I could see her lying on her side. I was told that early in the storm a large sloop near the entrance to the harbor had broken loose and swept up the harbor crashing into other boats and breaking them loose. Some of the boats along the shore had broken pennants hanging from their bows, and several had anchors with rodes attached to the bow to supplement the mooring anchor.

I then talked to Fred Coulson, who ran Barden's Boat Yard. He said they could get *Pearl III* off at high tide. The rise of the tide in Marion is only

Pearl III the Day after Hurricane Gloria

two feet and *Pearl III's* draft was 5-1/2' so she would still be aground at high tide. I then rowed out to *Pearl III* to survey the damage. It was all from other boats. The teak caprail was torn to pieces; the bow pulpit was badly bent, the turnbuckles were bent; one of the roller-furling extrusions was bent and the others had marks from the stays of other boats all the way to the top of the mast; and there were gouges and bad scrapes on both sides of the hull.

Later in the day at high tide Barden's took two powerboats out to *Pearl III*. She was still heeling badly in less than four feet of water. One of the boats took a halyard from the top of the mast out to the side. The other one took a line from the bow. Then they both went to full throttle, the one heeling *Pearl III* and the other one pulling her forward. Slowly she was moved into deeper water and finally was fully afloat. Once afloat she was taken to the dock and hauled for the winter. A great job! Now the problem was to get the repairs done in time for the next boating season. This would not be a simple matter because of the large number of boats with serious damage that had to be repaired.

Work in the spring proceeded slowly. By late May almost everything was done except for the teak caprail. More than half of the caprail had been damaged and had to be replaced. The carpenter doing the work was involved in a nasty divorce and was on the job infrequently. Although Barden's had a staff with the expertise required to do all the work, there was just too much for them to handle, so they had hired subcontractors. The carpenter was one of them. When only one piece at the bow remained to be fabricated and installed he failed to show up for about a week. This was too much for me to accept! I bought a piece of teak, made the piece to fit, and installed it myself. I then bolted on the new stainless bow fitting.

At this point everything was done except for installation of a new bow pulpit and a few other small items that were done quickly by Barden's crew.

There still was one remaining problem. The gelcoat repairs were unsatisfactory. It had been properly done but not properly finished – there were bad spots where the gelcoat had a rough texture rather than a smooth shiny finish. I knew there would be a long delay getting the original worker back to properly finish the job so I decided to do it myself. I talked to Fred Coulson and asked him how to do the job. He told me to start with 80 grit sandpaper and then use finer and finer paper, ending the job with polishing compound. I bought a new electric sander, sandpaper, and compound, and went to work. When I had finished polishing and waxing the hull it looked pretty good. When *Pearl III* was in the water it looked like new and any irregularities in the gelcoat were imperceptible.

The previous year in Maine we had planned to get a cabin heater for *Pearl III*, so I bought a Force 10-kerosene heater and mounted it on the port bulkhead over the end of the settee. It was not as cheery as having a wood fire in the Cole stove on *Pearl II,* but it was more convenient to use and did a good job heating the cabin.

By the end of the season we had some deck leaks, which I finally traced to the caprails. The carpenter had not used enough bedding compound when he installed them and there were leaks where they were screwed down. I removed the teak plugs and screws, filled the holes with caulking, replaced the screws, and put in new teak plugs. This reduced the leaks but didn't eliminate them. I concluded that they were coming from the screw holes that remained after the original caprail was removed, and could only be eliminated by removing the new caprail and starting over. Rather than do this we decided to live with the remaining leaks, which were not a serious problem.

In addition to the leak problem the carpenter did a poor job on the forward part of the caprail on the starboard side so it didn't quite match the rest of the caprail. This always annoyed me although I don't think any one else ever noticed it.

18
MAINE CRUISES 1986 and 1988

On Saturday August 9th 1986 we left Marion at 7:00 AM and made an overnight passage, arriving at McGlathery Island at 4:15 PM the next day. There was good wind for most of the time and we had nice stretches of sailing, with some motoring in between. Shortly after we anchored in the cove the *Idiot's Delight,* with Don and Anne Sullivan on board arrived. We had previously arranged to meet them there. Don had been the co-owner of *Scrimshaw* with Dick Stone and had bought another boat after they sold her. They rafted up with us and came aboard. It was a nice sunny day so we had cocktails in the cockpit. We invited a couple from *Heidi,* the only other boat in the cove, to join us. Six of us were comfortable in the cockpit with the tiller raised. *Heidi* was a Paine 30 footer that they, Ray and Barbara Voisine, had built from a bare hull. After cocktails the Voisines went back to *Heidi* and the Sullivans stayed for dinner and then untied from *Pearl III* and anchored. They left the next morning but we stayed. I put up the sail on the dinghy and circumnavigated McGlathery and Round islands. (I had rigged the dinghy for sailing shortly after we bought it). After returning from my sail I dug clams. I had a lot of trouble finding enough for chowder because the place had been dug over by commercial clammers.

Circumnavigating McGlathery Island

We went from McGlathery to Southwest Harbor, asked about a mooring at Beal's Lobster Pier on the north side of the harbor and were directed to a fisherman's empty mooring. The next morning I sailed the dinghy across the harbor to Hinkley's float and bought a new Chart Kit and two cushions.

We stayed in Southwest Harbor the rest of the day and rode our folding bikes into town for shopping, then we had lobsters at Beal's pier. Joyce thought it was a gross experience with no frills and no couth. Later in the evening I rode into town again and called John in California to inquire about some trouble he was having with the police over suspected drug dealers in his neighborhood.

Although they are close neighbors, Southwest Harbor is completely different from Northeast Harbor. Southwest Harbor is mostly a fishing port, whereas Northeast Harbor seems to cater more to cruising boats and yachtsmen.

From Southwest Harbor we went east past Schoodic and Petit Manan to Trafton Island. Nine large yachts were anchored there so we didn't stay. Instead we went around the north end of Dyer Island and anchored in Northeast Cove (see chart on page 144). This is a beautiful little spot between two small islands and Dyer Island. After anchoring we had two nice little steaks from Southwest Harbor. We stayed there overnight and then went east to Otter Cove on Moose Neck across from Cape Split. It's not a large harbor but by nightfall there were four other sailboats there.

The next day it rained all day and we stayed put, baked biscuits in the oven and had them with Dinty Moore Beef Stew enhanced with carrots, celery and other odds and ends. Joyce read "Letters of E. B. White" and I read a Spencer novel and a book about lobstermen loaned to me by Don Sullivan.

We left Otter Cove at 9:30 the next morning heading for Northeast Harbor 32 miles west. We motored in fog and drizzle and arrived at Clifton dock in the afternoon, got diesel and water and bought a 20-pound block of ice and two bags of cubes. The harbor was crowded because of the poor weather and talk of a hurricane, but we found an empty mooring. There was lots of hot water for showers and shampoos because of all the motoring. Dinner at the Popplestone; fresh salmon with egg sauce for Joyce and shrimp scampi for me!

From Northeast Harbor we headed west to Merchant Row in light wind, passed up McGlathery Island because of a mess of boats there, and went in to Hells Half Acre and anchored. A seal was swimming around in the water and ospreys were soaring around overhead.

The following morning we started out from Hells Half Acre in clear, bright, windless weather. It became overcast when we crossed West Penobscot Bay and headed for Tenants Harbor. South of Muscle Ridge Channel the current was running hard to the south. The area is peppered with lobster pots and their buoys were pulled under by the current and almost invisible, and we were motoring. Suddenly "BLAM!" the engine stopped and the bow slowly swung around to the south. Our propeller had hit a lobster pot buoy and we were anchored from the stern by the pot warp. Looking over the side I could see the warp extending diagonally from the stern. I got the boat hook and tried to pull it up but the current was too strong. Then I got out the lead line, dropped it down ahead of the warp, hooked it from the other side with the boat hook and pulled it up. I then pulled a half-inch nylon line down around the warp and up to the cockpit. I cleated one end of this line and wrapped the other end around a winch and winched up the warp up so I could cut it. We were free!

There was practically no wind so I was in the dinghy towing *Pearl III* when a motorboat came by, saw our plight, and towed us in to the outer part of Tenants Harbor near Long Cove. Once we were anchored I put on my swimming trunks and went over the side. There was a very large foam buoy, with a piece of the pot warp attached, jammed by the propeller into the aperture. I had no trouble getting it loose and into the cockpit. The name "B. Curtis" was engraved on the buoy. I was sorry to have cost B. Curtis a lobster pot and buoy, but had no choice.

Pot Buoy in Strong Current

Lobster Pot Buoys

The above photo to the left shows a lobster pot buoy being dragged under by strong current. The buoy of B. Curtis that gave us so much trouble is the large one with the white bottom in the photo to the right. The cut from the propeller is clearly visible.

We had a nice sail to Christmas Cove the next day, took our bikes ashore and peddled up and down hills until we finally found a grocery store at South Bristol, a little more than a mile from Christmas Cove. Following our bike ride we had drinks and a good dinner at the Coveside Restaurant. From Christmas Cove we had an uneventful trip home to Marion by way of Jewel Island, Gosport Harbor, and Provincetown.

In 1987 there was no Maine cruise. Our sailing activities were all local – Buzzards Bay and Martha's Vineyard. In August of 1988 we headed for Maine again. We left Marion at 4:45 PM on Monday August 15th and sailed to Bassetts Island with just the genoa in a southwest wind of 20 to 25 knots. In the morning I replaced the genoa with the yankee and we motored through the canal and sailed to the Race Point buoy in a 15 to 20 knot northwest wind. From there our destination was Matinicus Rock. The wind was variable until evening, when it gradually increased up to 28 knots from the northeast and I reduced sail to eventually just stays'l and mizzen. It turned out to be a wild night.

Joyce came on watch at midnight, having slept for several hours. Before going below she had been drinking a Coke and left the partly full can in a corner of the cockpit. When she came up she picked up the can, took a swig, and immediately threw up in the cockpit. The can was half full of salt water. The soup she had for a late snack had little pasta bow ties in it that looked like propellers, so for days after this we kept seeing these little propellers in the spaces in the cockpit grating.

In the morning the wind had shifted to north and gradually fell to about five knots. During the night I reached the conclusion that we couldn't make Matinicus Rock, so we changed course to Head Harbor at the south end of Isle au Haut. Then there were other wind shifts more favorable for Matinicus and we picked up a mooring there at 3:30 PM. We stayed overnight at Matinicus. The next day was bright and sunny with a north wind. We went ashore and walked the dirt roads. There were blueberry bushes and a few old cars and trucks along the sides of the road.

Matinicus Main Road   Harbor from Restaurant

We had lunch in a small restaurant overlooking the harbor – crabmeat sandwiches and blueberry pie with ice cream. (The next time we visited Matinicus the restaurant was gone.) After returning to the boat I got a bucket and went back and picked blueberries.

We left Matinicus at 2:45 PM and had a good sail to Head Harbor in a 15-25 knot NNW wind, dropping the anchor in 17 feet of water. It was a nice quiet spot. In the late evening two Outward Bound boats from Hurricane Island came in and anchored. There were 14 people on each boat. The night was cold and they spent it on the open boats huddled under tarps thrown over lines strung between the masts, while we were cozy below with our cabin heater running. In the morning we had blueberry pancakes with maple syrup for breakfast, then went ashore and collected smooth round popplestones.

Outward Bound Boat   Blueberry Pancakes

From Head Harbor we went to Stonington for supplies. We anchored and rowed ashore to a new public landing around the corner from Atlantic Hardware. All other docks had "No tying up!" signs on them. Stonington is the most inhospitable place on the Maine coast. We got supplies at Bartlett's Market. They had no ice and told us that Billing's Marine, a short distance west, had ice. We motored there and got two blocks and two bags of cubes, plus a new pressure switch for the fresh water system.

After Billings Marine we went to McGlathery Island. When we got there we were dismayed to find that our favorite anchoring spot was occupied by a fishing boat of some kind, so we anchored a bit farther out in the cove not far from it. Not only were they occupying our favorite spot, but also

Scallop Boat at McGlathery Island

they were playing a radio loudly and continually throwing overboard small things that came floating by us. I finally realized they were shucking scallops and throwing the shells overboard, so I got a plastic container, rowed over, and asked if I could buy some scallops. They asked, "Shelled or unshelled?" I returned to *Pearl III* with a plastic container full of really fresh (shelled) scallops for a very reasonable price. They were forgiven. For dinner: haddock, scallops, fried potatoes, and Beringer's Sauvignon Blanc – all delicious.

In the morning we walked across the clam-flats to the little green island and had a picnic lunch, walked around, and went back to the boat. The scallopers, who had left last night, were back playing their music and shucking their scallops so we left and went to Hells Half Acre. Shortly after we arrived another sailboat came in and anchored near Devil Island and then a Concordia yawl anchored nearby. They both were quiet and well behaved. I put the mast and sail on the dinghy and sailed around among the rocks for a while then went back to the boat and watched sailboats going east and west on Deer Island Thorofare. Dinner by Joyce: fish and scallop chowder, salad, and fruit compote of blueberries from Matinicus, bananas, and peaches. Another delicious meal!

The next morning I went for a sail in the dinghy, but had to paddle back when the wind died. Breakfast by Parker: orange juice, Jones sausages, fried eggs, heated coconut donuts, and coffee.

At 1:00 PM we left, headed east to Long Island. The weather was foul – north wind and rain, so I donned my foul weather gear and boots and took the helm while Joyce snuggled up under a warm blanket in the cabin. I picked up a red ball mooring in Lunt Harbor, rowed ashore and paid for the mooring, then ordered two 2 lb. Lobsters to be cooked by Lunt Deli and picked up at six. For dinner we had the last of the fish and scallop stew, lobsters, California Chardonnay, pound cake, and coffee. Dinner was accompanied by Mozart's "Symphonia Concertante".

The Lunt Deli   Chowder, Lobsters, and Chardonnay

We went ashore in the morning and walked across the island to Eastern Cove. The shore of the cove is a great berm of popplestones deposited there by the surf during storms. We sat on driftwood and ate lobster sand-wiches and drank beer that I had brought in a backpack. After lunch I collected symmetrical stones and but them in the backpack to take back to the boat. After returning to the boat through fir-tree fragrant woods we were told we could fill our water tanks, which we did. Old Mr. Lunt was standing on the dock and complained that the pleasure boats were draining the well up the hill. After filling the tanks and going back to the mooring we ate a spaghetti dinner on the boat and went to bed.

Frenchboro, Long Island

Eastern Cove Popplestones

The morning was cold and I lit the cabin heater to warm us up. We had French toast and sausages for breakfast and departed for Northeast Harbor. It was a beautiful day, but cold and windless when we left, and we motored all the way to Northeast Harbor (see chart on page 199). At Northeast Harbor we took our laundry to "Shirt off your Back", went to Brown's for charts, and the Pine Tree Market for groceries. Back at the boat I took a shower and we went ashore for dinner. The Popplestone was "Closed for the season". Their season ended pretty early! We found another small back-alley restaurant that was below average. The place was full of chil-dren sucking pacifiers and generally creating a ruckus. We were happy that we weren't saddled with any of them.

We awoke the next morning to find the *Amersee* moored right next to us. It belonged to Ken Eldred, a colleague of mine at Bolt Beranek and Newman. It was locked with no one aboard.

The forecast was for southeast winds at 25 to 30 knots, rain, fog, etc., so we left Northeast Harbor and went to Seal Cove on the west side of Mt. Desert Island, which would have good protection from the southeast. We motored out of Northeast Harbor, across Bass Harbor Bar and up Blue Hill Bay to the cove, where we anchored. There were two houses up on a cliff and one other boat anchored in the cove with no one aboard. We went exploring in the dinghy and rowed as far as we could go up a long creek that extends inland from the east end of the cove. When we got back we took the bikes ashore to a launching ramp and rode past a farm with five nervous horses that snorted and jumped when I went near them. Back to the boat, dinner, reading, and bed. Rain and gusty winds from 0 to 20 knots during the night.

In the morning it still was rainy, drizzly, and cold. We pulled up the anchor and motored up Bartlett Narrows to Galley Cove, a tiny cove at the northeast corner of Bartlett Island. We went ashore for a while and tramped around on the island. Back on the boat we just lolled around, read, and listened to music with the cabin heater on to warm the cabin and reduce the dampness.

The forecast had been for clearing and warmer weather, but in the morning there still was fog and drizzle. In spite of the bad weather we decided to go to Blue Hill. The wind was favorable for once, and we sailed all the way to Blue Hill. The inner harbor is very large and is scattered with ledges. The area near the town dries out at low tide and it is about a half mile to deeper water, where we anchored in 20 feet. After anchoring I rowed ashore to check out the town and to get ice. There was a wharf and a launching ramp, both of which dried out at low tide and left a wide mud flat that made it impossible to land. When I arrived it was half tide and I had no problem landing at the ramp.

Blue Hill Harbor

While ashore I came across the "Firepond", an interesting looking restaurant where we might have dinner. After returning to the boat I checked the tide tables and thought there would be enough water to land the dinghy on the ramp at 6:00 PM, At 5:45 we donned our foul weather gear (it was rainy and slightly foggy) and headed ashore in the dinghy. Concerned about poor visibility for the return voyage I took a small brass compass and we made a dogleg voyage to the shore; the first leg was to a small red sailboat and the second leg was to the ramp. I noted the compass course for each leg.

When we arrived at the head of the harbor the tide was still too low and there was mud for some distance out from the end of the ramp. We didn't reach the ramp until 7:00. When we did we put some small logs under the dinghy for rollers, hauled it to the top of the ramp, and tied it to an old trailer. The Firepond was booked up – except for one table. They led us downstairs and seated us by a window overlooking the bottom of a glade with a brook bubbling by right outside the window. It was a delightful spot. We had drinks and an excellent dinner. I had garlic soup and crab-meat pasta with cilantro, and Joyce had broccoli and mushroom soup and Mako shark. Desert was blueberry tarts – blueberries on a layer of vanilla sauce in a delicate crust, with whipped cream around the edges.

Although it was dark and the fog was thick when we left the restaurant, the trip back to *Pearl III* was a "piece of cake". The tide was high enough that it was easy to launch the dinghy and our reciprocal courses took us directly back to the little red sailboat and then to *Pearl III*. Without the compass and noted courses we might have been rowing around all night.

The Lighthouse on Green Island

We left Blue Hill the next morning planning to go to the Barred Islands by way of Eggemoggin Reach. We were using a new book, "A Cruising Guide to the Maine Coast" by Hank and Jan Taft. They said that the Barred Islands was a gorgeous spot. On the way to Eggemoggin Reach we passed a pretty little lighthouse on Green Island (also known as Frye

Island). The keeper's house and lighthouse were not high above the water and looked like they would be vulnerable in a storm.

In the reach there was no wind (the second time) and at the western end the fog set in thick. There were no navigational aids to help us get to the Barred Islands in thick fog so we anchored at Pickering Island, which was easy to find. The fog was lifting by the time we got to Pickering. We had chicken, rice, and fresh green beans for supper and then read in the cockpit, did the New York Times crossword puzzle, and went to bed,

In the morning we woke up with the boat listing to starboard. We were aground, thanks to our Signet depth sounder. It had given us trouble since the day we put the boat in the water. It frequently would freeze or quit just when it was needed most. I had sent it back to the factory and they didn't solve the problem. Anyway the tide was rising so there was no problem. The fog was thick so we stayed at Pickering for the day and night. For dinner we had a steak broiled in the oven, hash brown potatoes, and salad.

We left Pickering Island the next morning in dense fog that would lift enough now and then so islands could be made out here and there. The wind started out southwest at 12 to 15 knots and increased to 22 knots, at which time we were under reefed main and stays'l and decided to go to Pulpit Harbor. There were many boats and we anchored near the front of the fleet using our 35 lb. CQR and motoring it in. Then we went ashore and walked to "The Islander", a new store about two miles from the dock, came back, ate dinner, and went to bed.

We were awakened at 2:15 AM by heavy rain and gusting wind. I looked out one of the ports and everything seemed OK, but boats were swinging in all directions. I was looking out on the port side contemplating getting dressed and going out in the cockpit when I saw a boat heading towards us. I rushed on deck in my pajamas but was unable to fend it off. It was an Island Packet and had a long bowsprit and pulpit, which went through our pulpit on the port side, as shown in sketch "A" below.

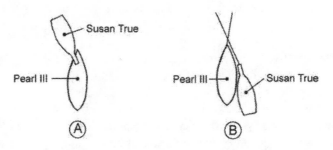

The skipper of the other boat, *Susan True,* stuck his head out of the companionway and said, "I'll get dressed and come out and help". I was able to get the pulpits apart by starting the engine and backing sharply to

port. The boats ended up side-by-side as shown in sketch "B", with the anchor rodes crossed and his over ours. I let out scope to bring us side-by-side. By this time the other skipper was dressed and on deck and while I was fending off he managed to get the bitter end of his rode under ours and Joyce was able to motor up to our anchor while I took in the rode. When we were right above the anchor I tried to pull it up but couldn't – it was dug in too deep. We motored it out and went across the harbor and picked up an empty mooring that I had seen the night before. I then watched Mr. Susan True pull up his anchor. He had so much scope out that it extended halfway across the harbor. When he had gotten it up I took *Pearl III* in to the dock to get water.

While at the dock I talked with Ross Thomas, who was in the cockpit of his Shannon 38 during the storm, and he said the boats were going in all directions. His own boat on a mooring did a complete 360-degree rotation. My conclusion was that the *Susan True,* with her long rode, swung completely around *Pearl III.* We'll never know, but the problem we had raising our anchor seems to indicate that we didn't drag. The only damage to either boat was bending of the bow pulpits. Mr. Susan True filed a claim against our insurance, but our agent told me they weren't going to pay it after reading my version of the incident. I straightened our bow pulpit using some 2x4's and heavy clamps.

From Pulpit Harbor we motored and sailed in a light southwest wind to Tenants Harbor, shopped for groceries, ice, and haddock, and had drinks and an excellent dinner at the East Wind Inn. The *Susan True* was there on a mooring!

At 9:30 the next morning we left Tenants Harbor under sail in a northwest wind of six to 8 knots, passed Burnt Island and Pemaquid Point, went north of Damariscove Island, and up the Sheepscot River to Ebenecook Harbor. As we entered Ebenecook Harbor *Susan True* came motoring down from the north, apparently having taken a different route, through Townsend Gut. There are three deep coves in Ebenecook Harbor, the first two being somewhat commercial and crowded. We went into the third one, Love Cove. We spent a quiet night with no wind. In the morning the water was glassy and two great blue herons were wading around near the shore. Love cove is a beautiful, well-sheltered secluded spot, except for two small houses nearby and a road passing the end of the cove.

We weighed anchor at 9:30 in the morning and sailed all the way to Jewel Island in a steady northwest wind of about 8 knots. No motoring for a change! We left Jewel at 6:30 the next morning under power in a light southwest wind. The wind started picking up at 8:00 and increased to 15 knots in the afternoon. It took several long tacks to get to Gosport Harbor, which we entered between Appledore and Smuttynose Islands (see chart on page 170). The harbor was crowded, it being Friday evening, but we found a mooring with a $10 sign on it across the harbor from the hotel. No one ever came to collect the $10.

Pancakes in the Cockpit

We left the mooring under power at 7:00 AM in order to have a favorable current in the Canal. At 8:30 we had coffee and pancakes in the cockpit. The wind was westerly all day, varying from 5 to 15 knots, so there was some sailing and some motoring. The wind in Buzzards Bay was southwest at 10 to 15 knots and we tacked to Marion under yankee, main, and mizzen.

At some time between the end of the boating season and the next spring we bought a small 12-volt television set with a built-in VCR. This required minor modifications to the forward corner of the main cabin on the starboard side, and installation of an outlet on the outside of the cabin for the antenna cable; a special antenna had to be hoisted up the main mast in order to use the television. We enjoyed the television and VCR during bad weather days when anchored or moored.

About this time ablative anti-fouling bottom paints came on the market. They lasted several seasons, eliminating the need to paint the bottom every year. The recommendation from the manufacturers was to apply two coats of different colors. When the first color began to show through it was time to repaint. I always did my own bottom painting so this sounded like a great idea. I applied two coats of Woolsey ablative paint. *When Pearl III* was hauled at the end of the boating season the bottom was covered with barnacles. I counted more than 100 barnacles on one square foot of the bottom. The news was that Woolsey had produced a faulty batch of bottom paint. I called Woolsey and they refused to pay for the cost of removing the barnacles and the faulty paint, which was a major project. They did offer to send new paint, but I never received any.

19

MISCELLANEOUS ADVENTURES 1989, 1990, 1991

In early August 1989 we headed for Maine again. We left Marion at 11:00 AM motoring to the canal. The boat seemed very sluggish and we realized we would not be able to reach the canal in time for a favorable current. We turned into the cove on the north side of Bassetts Island and anchored. I put on my swimming trunks and went over the side to check the propeller. It had a great wad of barnacles on it, so large that only the tips of the propeller were sticking out. I got back on the boat and got a screwdriver and an old plane blade that I kept for odd jobs like this one and then went back over the side and attacked the barnacles. It took about two hours, going up for air and back down every few minutes, but the propeller was finally free of barnacles. I had forgotten to polish the propeller before the boat was launched because of a number of other time-consuming chores that spring. Several years before I had stopped using a zinc because it was inviting barnacles, and polishing the prop had done the job for several previous years. When we left Bassetts the next morning under power the boat was back to its normal speed.

On this same trip we had a visitor during our offshore passage to Maine. A little bird landed in the cockpit beside the mizzenmast. It sat there for a while and then flew up to the cabin top and rested there in several places before it finally took off to the west, probably heading for land.

A Visitor at Sea

On our 1990 cruise we went to Seal Bay on Vinalhaven Island for the first time. This is a large bay with many ledges and many good anchoring places. The entrance is tricky, between rocks and ledges, but once inside it provides delightful, well-protected anchorages that are worth the effort of getting in. We saw a seal in the water and an Outward Bound student ashore. Part of the school's training is to put a student ashore in some remote spot, where he/she is required to take care of his/her self alone for several days before being picked up.

Seal Bay

In 1990 we finally got to the Barred Islands, which we failed to do in a previous year because of fog. We sailed there from Rockport in nice weather. It was a tight anchorage between a group of small islands – pretty, but no more so than many other Maine anchorages we had visited. The adventure came the next day after we left the anchorage in dense fog. We were motoring slowly and Joyce was on watch with the autopilot on. We were in open water and the only thing to watch for was other boats. Suddenly Joyce shouted and I rushed out into the cockpit to see a huge powerboat moving at high speed right towards us. I turned off the autopilot and threw the tiller to starboard as far as it would go, which got us out of their path. The boat had two radar antennas revolving and a uniformed lookout standing on the bow. If I hadn't reacted quickly they would have cut us in two. The lookout on the bow acted as if he had not even seen us, and they continued on their way, still at high speed. Joyce said she would never come back to Maine unless we had radar.

That same year we stopped overnight behind the breakwater at Richmond Island. I entered the harbor too close to the north shore of the island and ran into the reefs there. It was a bad jolt but we bounced right off. When the boat was hauled in the fall there was a big piece of lead missing from the forward corner of the keel. I put some stainless crews into the keel as anchors, and replaced the missing lead with loaded epoxy.

The next spring I bought a small radar. Before the boat was launched I mounted the antenna on the mizzenmast and the receiver by the chart table in the cabin. Then I snaked the cable down the mast, cut it off, and snaked the other piece down under the cockpit and up in the cabin to the receiver. The next step was to solder the cable wires to the two parts of a connector at the bottom of the mast. There must have been 20 little wires that had to be soldered to 20 little pins on each side, a painstaking task. When the boat was rigged and in the water the radar didn't work. I assumed there was a problem with my soldering job, so the next weekend I took some 2x4's, big clamps, and an automobile jack to the boat. After loosening the stays and clamping the 2x4's on the mast I was able to use the jack to lift the mast and get at the connector. I examined the soldering job on both sides with a magnifying glass and discovered a piece of solder bridging between two wires, and voila! After eliminating the bridge the radar worked.

Most years cruising in Maine we visited some harbors and anchorages we hadn't been to before. In 1991, as in 1990, we went to several new places. At Kennebunkport we visited an old high school friend of Joyce's on our way east. We motored up the Kennebunk River and got a slip at Chick's Marina. It was the only time *Pearl III* would ever be at a slip.

Another new anchorage that year was Damariscove Island. The harbor is almost two miles long and less than 200' wide. There is an abandoned Coast Guard station at the entrance to the harbor. To prevent swinging into the shore on either side we put down a stern anchor. In spite of its small size Damariscove Harbor was a major maritime port in the early 17th century, with as many as 30 vessels riding at anchor.

Damariscove Harbor   *Pearl III* at Damariscove

In August the Charles River Power Squadron held a rendezvous at the summer home of one of the members on Lineken Bay, just east of Booth-bay. We planned to go there and anchor, then row ashore to the rendez-vous. The weather the day of the rendezvous was very nasty, with high winds and rain. The location was at the northwest corner of the bay. We motored up to what we thought was the right place, but there were no other boats there and we couldn't see any activity ashore. We motored around in the miserable weather in our foul weather gear and boots and concluded it was too nasty to anchor at that location. I checked the chart and found a small cove (Perch Cove) on the western shore of the bay that had good protection from the southeast wind, so we went over and anchored and spent a comfortable night. We learned later that only a few people went to the rendezvous, and none went by boat.

Hurricane Island

We went to Hurricane Island and picked up a guest mooring, rowed ashore, and toured the island. The island is the home of the "Hurricane Island Outward Bound School". The school teaches young people outdoor activities and self-reliance. In the 19th century Hurricane Island was a thriving community with a post office, store, and living facilities for as many as 1,200 Italian immigrants engaged in quarrying, shaping, and finishing granite. The remains of these operations are still scattered around the island. The school uses the old quarry for teaching rock climbing skills.

Granite Quarry   Old Granite Machinery

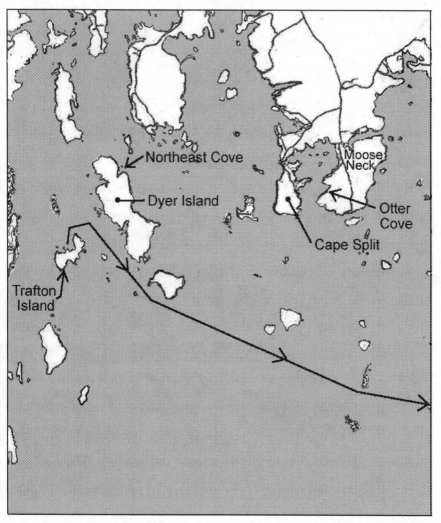

From Trafton Island

The most exciting part of our 1991 cruise was Hurricane Bob. We were anchored at Trafton Island and Hurricane Bob was moving up the coast. We had to get to a hurricane hole before it reached us. We headed for the Mudhole, which was a perfect spot and was only 18 miles away. We left Trafton Island in dense fog making good use of radar and loran, motored southeast past many ledges to just beyond a bell at Seahorse Rock, and then turned on a course that would take us just south of a series of large

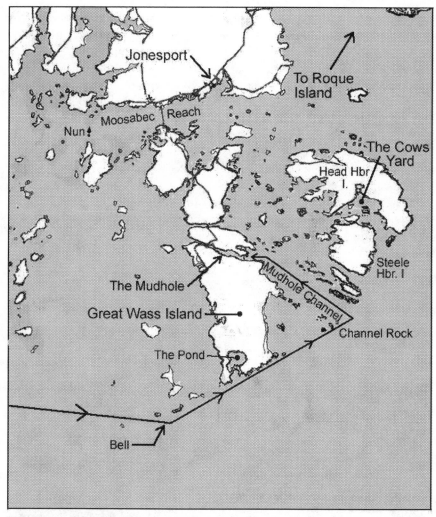

To the Mudhole

rocks and the rocky coast of Great Wass Island. When we got just beyond
Channel Rock we turned up the Mudhole Channel until we reached the
entrance to the Mudhole. At that point we could dimly see a protrusion of
land from Great Wass Island. We had traveled 18 miles past ledges, rocks,
and Great Wass Island without seeing anything until then but one bell
buoy. We could, however, see it all on the radar screen.

Fortunately we arrived at the Mudhole at a time when the tide was high enough so we could get in over the ledges at the entrance. We motored to the middle of the Mudhole and anchored near a small white buoy. Shortly after we anchored a small wooden sailboat towing a motorized dory came in. The owner, Nathaniel Rowe, notified us that the buoy was his winter mooring and would we please move, which we did. He said he had kept his boat there safely for many winters except for one year when someone shot a hole in it and it sank. He had to have it raised and towed out for repairs. He said, "This is the only boat that was sunk by gunfire in these waters for the last 200 years". He then got in his dory and motored out of the harbor.

Shortly after he left a lobster boat came in and rafted up on the port side of his boat and the occupants rowed ashore. Then another lobster boat came in and rafted up and they rowed ashore. The lobstermen on both boats had rowed lines ashore and tied them to trees. After they left I prepared for the blow by stripping off the sails and anything else above decks that might blow away or increase the windage.

Pearl III at the Mudhole Prepared for Hurricane Bob

Several other sailboats came in and anchored, making a total of seven boats in this small harbor. I contemplated putting out a stern anchor but decided it would be better to let the boat swing with the wind.

I had been tracking the path of the storm and plotting it on a chart and it appeared that it would pass far to the west of our location This proved to be correct and the highest wind speed I clocked on our windmeter was 40 knots. I must note that I got much better information about the location of the storm from the local radio station than I did from NOAA.

During the night the small stern anchor of one of the sailboats, a Cape Dory 36, let go and it swung into another sailboat. I flashed a searchlight at them and they eventually appeared in the cockpit. The anchor rodes of the two boats were entwined and they had quite a time getting them apart. There was no one on the other boat.

Rafted Boats at the Mudhole   The Entrance to the Mudhole

Nathaniel Rowe came back in the morning and was not too happy about the lobster boats rafted up to his. He said he had put the mooring in 20 years ago, but for some unknown reason the lobstermen thought it was theirs.

We left the Mudhole towing the dinghy. When we turned west after leaving Mudhole Channel I realized that I hadn't bailed the dinghy, which was full of water and was towing badly, lurching from side to side. The wind was east and I wanted to turn north at the west end of Great Wass Island to stop and bail the dinghy where there would be shelter. Immediately after turning north we were confronted by an unbroken line of nasty looking submerged ledges barely showing above the water, so I made a hasty U-turn and went back out. I checked the chart and found that I hadn't gone far enough – instead of turning at the end of Great Wass Island I had turned into "The Pond", which is completely blocked by ledges (see chart on page 145). After this scary incident we just continued on our way (with the waterlogged dinghy lurching along behind us) to Northeast Harbor, where I bailed it.

On this same trip, for the first time ever, there was no mooring available at Inner Winter Harbor. We went out to Sand Cove, which is not nearly as well protected. I had to put out a stern anchor to head *Pearl III* into the swells and prevent rolling. In the morning we put the outboard on the Perrywinkle and motored our bikes ashore to the yacht club float, then rode up the hill to Chase's restaurant and had a bacon and egg breakfast.

On one leg of our return trip from Maine to Marion we left Jewel Island in the morning at daybreak. After passing to the west of Jewel and Inner Green Islands we saw Halfway Rock* Lighthouse to the east just as the sun was approaching the horizon. A rare opportunity and quite a beautiful sight.

Halfway Rock Lighthouse at Sunrise

Before and during Hurricane Bob we had wished that *Pearl III was* safe at home in Marion, where we could have had her hauled. We changed our minds when we got back to Marion. Many boats stayed on their moorings and some of them broke loose and were up on the land. Barden's had hauled a lot of boats and put them on jackstands in the adjacent field. They fared no better than those that stayed on their moorings. Although the field was well about the high water mark, the surge from the storm was so high (about eight feet) that it floated many boats off the jackstands and they crashed into each other causing serious damage to many of them. The storm was so bad that big doors on Barden's sheds were ripped off and deposited out on the street. So luck was with us this time. We were much better off in the Mudhole than we would have been in Marion, even if *Pearl III* had been hauled.

*Halfway Rock had a history of terrible shipwrecks before a light was finally established there in 1869. When the brig *Samuel* struck the rock in a nasty southeast gale the captain and steward were washed overboard and drowned. Fishermen from Hope Island saw the crew's distress signals and **rowed 5 miles** to their rescue. The last wreck was on February 12, 1861. Masses of wreckage washed up on Jewell and Inner Green Islands. The British bark *Boadicia* had smashed hard on the rock and all hands were drowned.

John Hughes' House after Bob   *Pearl III* Safe at Home Port

In the early spring I ordered a "Sailtainer" and a fully battened main to go with it. This allowed the mainsail to roll up partway in the boom for reefing, or all the way for storage. This was easily done from the cockpit with the halyard and a furling line. To reef or furl the sail the halyard was eased and the furling line pulled in, rolling the sail into the boom the desired amount. It created a perfect reef when rolled to one of the full-length battens. Installation of the system required riveting a special track to the mast, cutting the existing gooseneck from the mast, and bolting on a special gooseneck fitting.

At the end of 1991 we bought an inflatable Avon dinghy and outboard motor. The dinghy could be rolled up and stored in a cockpit locker for offshore passages and then inflated when we reached our destination, thereby eliminating the need to hoist the Perrywinkle aboard and lash it down on the deck.

After using the Avon for a while, and pumping it up every weekend when we often didn't use it except to get to from the dock to *Pearl III* and back, I designed and built a "little" plywood dinghy and made wooden davits for it. It would stay on the davits and be there if we needed it to go ashore. For weekend cruises we would leave the Avon at home and use Barden's launch to get to and from *Pearl III*. (see chapter 24 for more information about the Avon and the little plywood dinghy).

20
1992 and 1993 RENDEZVOUS AND CRUISES

In the spring of 1992 I purchased and installed Adler-Barber refrigeration and added two inches of foam insulation in the icebox. Because of the constant current drain I also added a high-capacity alternator and four six-volt golf cart batteries in place of the two 12-volt marine batteries. I also installed instrumentation to monitor the state of the batteries in order to know when to switch from one bank to the other and when to run the engine for charging. We had to run the engine at least one hour every day. We could now take frozen foods and make our own ice cubes. The only disappointment was that the refrigerator would not keep ice cream frozen.

I was elected commander of the Charles River Power Squadron at the Change of Watch in March. Since we were a boating organization one of my goals was to have at least one rendezvous where members could get together on their boats and ashore. I began planning a rendezvous at Red-brook Harbor on Buzzards Bay where we could get together and have din-ner ashore at the Chart Room. When they heard about it members Ed and Martha Roney offered their summerhouse, which overlooked the harbor, as headquarters for the rendezvous.

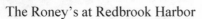

The Roney's at Redbrook Harbor   The Harbor from the Roney's

Many members went to the rendezvous in boats and others arrived in cars and slept in tents they pitched on the Roney's property. We had dinner Friday evening at the Chart Room and other meals at the Roney's, includ-ing Sunday morning breakfast before we left for home. Saturday there was an auction of nautical articles donated by members of the squadron. Our friends and former members, Jerry and Ann Schwarzkopf were up from Florida and we invited them to sail to the rendezvous with us and stay on

Pearl III for Friday and Saturday nights. The Redbrook Harbor rendezvous was a great success and it became a tradition for many years.

Boats at the Rendezvous

Jerry and Ann on *Pearl III*

Watching the Auctioneer

Dinner at the Roney's

We had one other weekend rendezvous in 1992. This one was by boat only. We first met in Tarpaulin Cove where we ate dinner on the boats and then sailed to Cuttyhunk to join a rendezvous being held by the USPS District. We had a cookout on the beach at the south side of the channel leading into Cuttyhunk pond. As I remember there were about five boats. We went to Maine after the Rendezvous but visited no new places.

In 1993 we had another successful rendezvous, this one at the summer home of members Bill and Linda McCabe in Cushing, Maine. The house overlooks Maplejuice Cove and there is a float for landing dinghies.

We left Marion at 11:40 AM Wednesday the 28th of July, motored through the canal and sailed in a nine-knot east wind to the Race Point bell, where the wind died. We motored off and on through the night. When we entered the St. George River the next day the fuel pump quit. With no motor our progress up the river was painfully slow against an adverse current in light wind. At times I thought we would have to anchor to prevent going backwards. We eventually reached the McCabe's, anchored and rowed ashore. A power squadron member loaned me a car and I drove to Rockland for a replacement fuel pump.

The rendezvous officially started Friday evening and lasted through Sunday. There were cocktails on the deck, a clambake on the grass, an auction on the deck, and breakfast in the garage (because of inclement weather).

McCabe's Dock and House

Bill and Linda McCabe

Waiting for the Auction

Auctioneer Rick Amerault

Once again Jerry and Ann Schwarzkopf were up from Florida. They drove to the rendezvous, but stayed with us on *Pearl III* at night. Like the Redbrook Harbor rendezvous this one became a tradition and was repeated for several years.

Monday morning we left the McCabe's after filling our water tanks at the dock. New places we visited were Cradle Cove and Grindel Point. Cradle Cove is on the east side of 700 Acre Island in West Penobscot Bay. We motored across Gilkey Harbor to Islesboro trying to find the Islesboro Inn, but the float said, "Private Keep Off" (we guessed that the inn had been sold and was closed). We then motored up to the east side of Grindel Point, anchored and took our bikes ashore for a five mile ride along the west side of Islesboro Island. This was an enjoyable ride on a relatively level road in pleasant weather.

We had an interesting visit at Inner Winter Harbor. We motored around the harbor looking for a mooring when we saw someone waving at us from a sailboat rafted up to a lobster car. We motored over and they said to raft up on the other side. Their boat was named *Breaking Away* and there were four people aboard. The harbormaster said they could stay there overnight.

Pearl III and *Breaking Away* at Inner Winter Harbor

Lobster Dinner on a Lobster Car

As we were rafting up on the other side of the lobster car they were rearranging empty lobster crates into a table and four seats, and then they proceeded to eat their lobster dinner on the lobster car.

On this cruise we stopped overnight between Hall and Harbor Islands, an anchorage Paul Duggan had told us about. We picked up a small white buoy labeled "Mooring" to differentiate it from the lobster pot buoys. There is a small house on Harbor Island and the owners invite people to come ashore and walk the paths around the island, which is populated with wildflowers and berry bushes. We rowed ashore in the Avon and walked the paths and picked and ate raspberries.

On this same cruise we went to Winter Harbor on Vinalhaven Island. This is a narrow slot on the east side of the island just north of Seal Bay. It is similar to Damariscove – long and narrow. We anchored between the second island and the cliff to the north, as indicated on the chart on page 206. Four other boats came in to this little harbor and anchored after we did, one by the first island, two behind us, and one farther in.

Joyce and the Avon Inflatable Dinghy at Harbor Island

At the end of the cruise we stopped in at Christmas Cove, deflated and rolled up the dinghy on their float, and stored it in the cockpit locker. Our route back from this cruise was from Christmas Cove to Marion. We left at 7:20 the next morning. The sea was lumpy for most of the voyage with a southeast wind of 10 to 15 knots. At around midnight a square-rigger passed by on the port side heading in the opposite direction. It was like a ghost ship in the dark.

Early in the morning the wind shifted more to the east and we had several hours of excellent sailing at six to seven knots. We picked up our mooring in Marion at 12:58 PM.

21
1994 THROUGH 2001

During these years we took our usual weekend cruises in Buzzards Bay and vicinity and went to Maine almost every year. Most of our Maine cruises were to familiar harbors and anchorages. We never missed our favorite spots: McGlathery Island, Tenants Harbor, Christmas Cove, and Inner Winter Harbor.

At the end of the sailing season in 1995 we had serious engine problems. One of the cylinders was not getting adequate fuel and the engine was irregular. I took the injector pump to an outfit that specialized in diesel engine repair and they told me it should be rebuilt. They rebuilt it during the winter. After the boat was launched in the spring the engine still was not working well and I discovered that the number four cylinder was not firing. I talked to Barden's mechanic about this and he said to remove the head and bring it to him, which I did. In about five minutes he found the problem. The valve stem on number four was bent. He replaced the valve and also did a complete valve job. At the same time I worked on the cooling water system. I shortened and rerouted the cooling-water hoses, eliminating some of the fittings and sharp bands in the system. This solved a chronic overheating problem when motoring at full throttle that had existed from the time we bought the boat. Once the head was reinstalled we could motor at seven knots for extended periods of time if needed.

During this period of time we visited two anchorages in Maine we had not visited before. One of the new places was Robinhood in Georgetown. We motored up the Sheepscot River and then the Little Sheepscot River, which is a narrow passage between Georgetown and Macmahan Islands. At the north end of this passage there is a torturous turn to the west through a narrow part of Gooseneck Passage, then to the northwest, and finally westerly to Robinhood Marina. When we followed this route the tidal current was running strong and rapid turns of the tiller were required to stay on course. We got a mooring from Robinhood Marina and went ashore for dinner at "The Osprey" Restaurant.

The other new place was Perry Creek on the south side of Fox Islands Thorofare. This is well-protected anchorage where we had tried to anchor several years before, but were unable to because it was too crowded. This time we did find room and anchored, but thought it was not worth the trouble. Although it was a beautiful spot there were just too many boats.

For many years we had been picking up the white pole mooring in Gosport Harbor that I had first used on my hectic ride on *Pearl II* in 1978. It had a sign on it that said, "Private Property No Trespassing". My thinking about this was that if the owner didn't show up there would be no problem, and if he did show up I could move. One of the times we picked up this mooring we were sitting in the cockpit on a nice evening having cocktails when an old fishing boat pulled up on the starboard side. The skipper said, "You're on my mooring." I told him I would move and headed for the bow. He said, "You don't have to move. I'll just hang off your stern for the night if it's OK with you. I'll be leaving very early in the morning", which he did. So much for scary messages on private moorings!

In 1995 we had an interesting experience because of Hurricane Felix, which was headed for North Carolina. It was not a threat to New England, but it was causing huge swells where we were in Maine. We sailed from McGlathery Island planning to anchor and spend the night in the cove on the north side of Burnt Island in Muscongus Bay (see picture on page 120). When we got there it was a raging terror with huge swells and waves crashing on the shore. In no way could we anchor and stay there. We would have to motor to Port Clyde, which was the nearest good harbor, and it was getting dark. The way in to Port Clyde would be peppered with lobster pot buoys just waiting to latch on to our propeller. The surf was crashing on Old Cilley Ledge, which we passed, and on numerous other ledges surrounding us on our five-mile passage, and we felt that we were in a desperate situation because of the lobster pot buoy problem.

Quiet Water in Port Clyde the Morning After

When it got dark we used a searchlight trying to avoid lobster pot buoys. As we entered Port Clyde the visibility was terrible and we had a lot of difficulty finding a mooring. We finally found one and settled back with good stiff drinks to decide what to do in the morning. There were no swells in Port Clyde and we spent a quiet night.

The next morning Joyce announced that she'd had enough and was going to jump ship and fly to Boston. We called Knox County Airport and made a reservation on Colgan Airways. In the afternoon I put her in a taxi and off she went, leaving me to make a single-handed overnight passage to Marion

I got up at the crack of dawn the next morning and made myself a big breakfast of eggs, sausages, fried potatoes, toast, and coffee. As I sat down to eat I said to myself, "The condemned man ate a hearty meal." I motored out of Port Clyde at 6:25 AM in thick fog with no wind. By 8:00 the fog had lifted and the wind was northwest at six to eight knots and I sailed for a while, but there was very little wind for most of the day and night so I motored most of the time. At night I turned the radar so I could see the screen from the starboard settee where I slept. I set the radar alarm so a boat that came close would set it off, and set my alarm watch to go off every half-hour so I could check the radar. With this arrangement I spent a fairly comfortable night.

At 6:15 AM the wind picked up from the southeast and from then on I sailed, except for the passage through the Cape Cod Canal. In Buzzards Bay the wind was 20 the 30 knots and I made a fast passage to Marion, where I picked up the mooring at 1:52 PM. Not a bad experience after all!

In 1999 Joyce's younger sister Dorothy and her Husband John Cook moved from Tennessee to Falmouth, near Quissett Harbor. From then on we frequently sailed to Quissett Harbor on weekends and picked up a mooring, Then went ashore and walked to their nearby house, where we had dinner and stayed overnight. Dorothy had Parkinson's disease and wasn't getting out much, so she and John were happy to have our company.

There were some interesting experiences on our Maine cruise in 2000. We had a nice sail to Scituate, but the next morning the wind was 20 to 30 knots from the northeast. We headed out of the harbor but went right back in because of the high wind on the nose and the heavy sea. The forecast was for the same winds the next day plus occasional rain. I rigged the canopy like a tent forward and level towards the stern. With this arrangement we could sit in the cockpit out of the wind and rain. We spent a lot of time reading and watching TV. After two days we left with the wind still northeast but at only 10 knots. We went to the Isles of Shoals, Jewel Island, and Christmas Cove. At Christmas Cove we had a good dinner at Coveside; clam chowder, baked haddock, blueberry pie and ice cream.

Going east from Christmas Cove we stopped at Tenants Harbor; McGlathery Island; and Lunt Harbor, Long Island. Along the way I discovered that my credit card was missing so I called Coveside, where I had used it last. They had it so we would stop there on our way west to pick it up

The Windjammer *Grace Bailey*

Sailing between McGlathery Island and Lunt Harbor we came across the windjammer *Grace Bailey* (see chart on page 195). The wind was light and we were able, literally, to "sail circles" around her to get views from all angles. Then the wind picked up and she took off leaving us in her wake.

On our return trip we stopped at Christmas Cove to pick up my credit card. We called the Duggans and when they arrived we had cocktails on the deck and then went in to an excellent dinner, as usual. From there we planned to go to Jewel Island, the Isles of Shoals, Scituate, and then Marion.

When we got to Gosport Harbor at the Isles of Shoals it was "wall to wall" boats. Absolutely no place to moor or anchor. We should have known better than to try to stop there on a weekend in good weather! We left Gosport Harbor and headed for Annisquam. The wind was 10 to 15 knots on the nose. We tacked until we were six miles from Annisquam then motored the rest of the way. At Annisquam we picked up a mooring near the yacht club. The launch driver came over and said there would only be four feet of water at low tide, but there were no other moorings available. He suggested that we go to Rockport, Mass, but we weren't about to do that since the Cruising Guide said the moored boats were so close together you could walk across them to get to shore. So we stayed on the mooring. I had checked the depth and the tide table and I thought we would have enough water at low tide. Not so!

We woke up at 2:00 AM with the keel rubbing on the sandy bottom. I tried motoring in order to get to deeper water but was not able to move more than a boat length, so there we stayed. I told Joyce that *Pearl III* would be heeling only a small amount and there was no danger. We should go back to bed until about 3:45 when the tide would be rising and that we should be upright by 4:00. She was not convinced and stayed awake huddled under a blanket until 3:45 when the boat began to right itself. Shortly after 4:00 we were upright and on our way.

We took two days to get back to Marion, stopping overnight at Scituate. After we rounded Bird Island and were heading into Marion harbor a small outboard motorboat full of teenagers approached from the opposite direction. As they neared us on the port side they slowed and one of them shouted, "Do you have any Grey Poupon?" Then they all laughed and sped off towards Buzzards Bay.

22
AN ELECTRONIC CRUISE

Our navigation equipment for our Maine cruise in 2002 was a far cry from the equipment on our first two cruising boats. The Alacrity and *Snoopy* had only a compass, a lead line, and paper charts. *Pearl III* now had a compass, a depth sounder, a knot-log, a wind meter, radar, GPS, a laptop computer, and electronic and paper charts. The radar allowed us to see other boats, buoys, and land masses in dense fog and at night; the GPS gave our position within 10 feet and provided steering instructions when programmed with course data. Each day I was able to plot a course on the computer with numerous waypoints and transfer the information to the GPS. The GPS could then display the heading to the first waypoint. When each waypoint was reached the GPS would automatically switch the heading to the next one.

Using Microsoft Word I designed an electronic log with a daily checklist and the ability to insert a narrative and digital photos. I also plotted the courses on paper charts as a backup in the event that there was an electronics failure.

As illustrated in the following photos, the laptop could be pivoted to be seen from the chart-table seat or from the cockpit. It also could be closed and slid back over the quarter berth for storage.

Laptop beside the Chart Table Seat

Laptop from Cockpit   Laptop Stored

The original electronic log had only one page for each day. If there was room on the page a picture from a digital camera was edited to fit using Photoshop Elements, and then imported to the log. Several additions have been made for the book, including more pictures, simplified charts, and stories about some of the lighthouses pictured.

The Electronic Cruise begins on the next page.

A MAINE CRUISE
ON PEARL III

Joyce and Parker Hirtle
July 24 to August 15, 2002

Day and Date: *Wednesday July 24, day 1 - Marion*

Check List:

Water 1: *Full*	**Battery 1:** *12.4*
Water 2: *Full*	**Battery 2:** *12.4*
CNG 1: *300*	**Fuel:** *3/4*
CNG 2: *Full*	**Holding Tank:** *Empty*
Log: *000*	**Engine hrs:** *1670*

Problems: *Arrived in Marion about 8 PM. P out to bring boat in to dock to load up. Engine stalled and would not start right after leaving mooring. Had to anchor. Bled injector pump – air in line. Bled injectors. Started engine again and got in to dock. We decided to stay there overnight and talk to Dennis (Barden's Foreman) about the problem in the morning because this same problem had occurred the last time we were on the boat, and we can't afford to have it happen in the canal.*

Marion Harbor

Day and Date: *Thursday July 25, day 2 - Marion to Scituate*

Check List:

Water 1: *Full*	**Battery 1:** *12.4*
Water 2: *Full*	**Battery 2:** *12.4*
CNG 1: *300*	**Fuel:** *3/4+*
CNG 2: *Full*	**Holding tank:** *Empty*
Log: *000*	**Engine hrs:** *1670*

Problems: *Motor stalling. P talked to Dennis at 7 AM. He asked if we had a Racor filter and said they were notorious and there probably was an air leak. The mechanic would be in at 7:30 and he'd send him over. P already had checked hose fittings for leaks, then discovered there was a drop of fuel at the Racor drain plug, and tightened the plug. The mechanic came and checked everything out. Said everything seemed to be OK, and that the fuel pump could have sucked air through the tiny leak at the bottom of the filter.*

Weather: *Sunny. Wind NE 10-15. Was lower at times during the day.*

Navigation: *Plotted daily routes on the computer each morning and transferred them to the GPS. Also plotted the courses on charts so that we had a backup in case of problems with the GPS, and also so we could check where we were from time to time. Departed Marion at 8:15 AM heading for Scituate. Motored through canal. Put up sails at end of canal. Close hauled most of the way. Sea very lumpy. Not a comfortable sail. Arrived in Scituate Harbor at 4:45 PM. Met by Satuit Boat Club launch. Got mooring for $25.*

Comments: *Cocktails on board. Chicken and pasta for dinner. White wine. Watched "Anatomy of a Murder" video. Didn't get to bed until midnight.*

Scituate Harbor Light

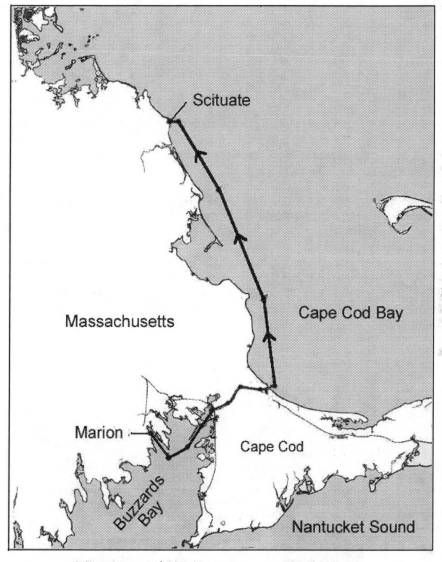

Marion to Scituate - 45 Miles

Day and Date: *Friday July 26, day 3 – Scituate*

Check List

Water 1: *In use 1 day*	**Battery 1:** *12.2*
Water 2: *Full*	**Battery 2:** *12.4*
CNG 1: *300*	**Fuel:** *3/4*
CNG 2: *Full*	**Holding tank:** *3/4 full*
Log: *45*	**Engine hrs:** *1674*

Weather: *Sunny. Wind NE 10-15. Temp 65F.*

Navigation: *Headed out at 8 AM – destination Gosport Harbor. Sea very lumpy. Boat pitching up and down. Would be a nasty beat almost all the way tacking back and forth. Turned around and returned to Scituate for the day. Will leave tomorrow morning, weather permitting.*

Comments: *Ran engine for an hour in the morning after aborted departure. Batteries up to 12.8. Loafed around until 3:30 PM then went ashore. Satuit launch lands at the north end of the harbor, which is quite far from the center of town. We walked to post office, which is several miles out of town in the opposite direction, then had dinner at the Mill Wharf Restaurant. Good martini, roasted scrod, garlic-mashed potatoes, vegetables, and mile high ice cream pie shared for dessert. Went to grocery store after dinner for milk, sugar, muffins, and sandwich meat, then back to boat by a different launch that we got near the Mill Wharf Restaurant.*

Satuit Boat Club

Thatcher Island

Thatcher Island is located off the east coast of Cape Ann and can be seen on the passage from Scituate to the Isles of Shoals. When the lighthouses were built in 1789 flashing lights were not in use, and two towers were built for easy identification. The two towers were in use until 1932 when the south light was electrified by means of a 6,000' submarine cable to the mainland. At that time the south light became flashing red and the north light was extinguished.

Day and Date: *Saturday July 27, day 4 - Scituate to Isles of Shoals*

Check List:

Water 1: *In use 2 days*   **Battery 1:** *12.2*
Water 2: *Full*   **Battery 2:** *12.2*
CNG 1: *250*   **Fuel:** *3/4*
CNG 2: *Full*   **Holding tank:** *7/8 full*
Log: *45*   **Engine hrs:** *1675*

Weather: *Overcast. Wind SE 0-5*

Navigation: *Departed Scituate under power at 6:15 AM heading for Cape Ann. Sea lumpy. Motored to Cape Ann and then to Gosport Harbor. Arrived at Gosport Harbor 3:15 PM. Picked up red ball mooring in location where white pole used to be. Motored all the way. Not many boats. Total about 20 by evening.*

Comments: *Up about 5:45 AM to get an early start because it is almost 50 miles to the Isles of Shoals. Muffins and coffee for breakfast. Pumped holding tank about 7:30 AM.*

White Island Light at the Isles of Shoals

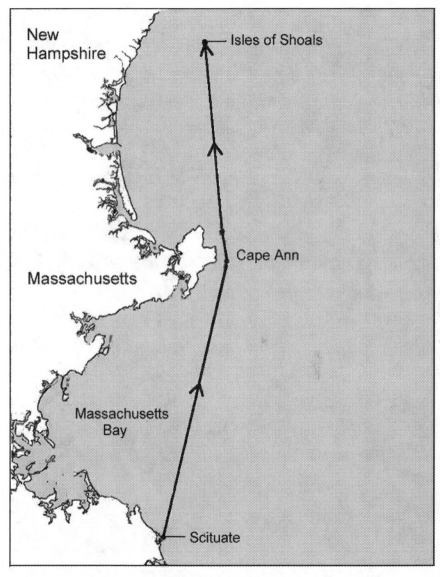

New
Hampshire

Isles of Shoals

Cape Ann

Massachusetts

Massachusetts
Bay

Scituate

Scituate to Isles of Shoals - 48 Miles

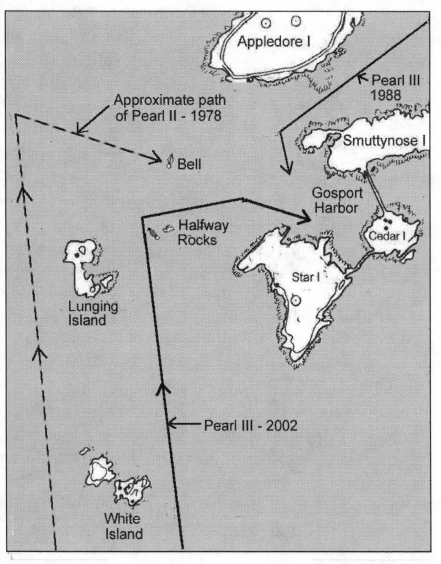

Appledore I

Pearl III
1988

Approximate path
of Pearl II - 1978

Bell

Smuttynose I

Gosport
Harbor

Halfway
Rocks

Cedar I

Lunging
Island

Star I

Pearl III - 2002

White
Island

To Gosport Harbor

Early Morning at Gosport Harbor

Day and Date: *Sunday July 28, day 5 - Isles of Shoals to Jewel Island*

Check List:

Water 1: *In use 3 days*   **Battery 1:** *12.5*
Water 2: *Full*   **Battery 2:** *12.2*
CNG 1: *Ran out today*   **Fuel:** *3/41*
CNG 2: *1800*   **Holding tank:** *1/3*
Log: *93*   **Engine hrs:** *1684*

Problems: *At about 1:30 PM there was a loud clack-clack noise from the engine. P loosened injector on No. 1 and it stopped; started again when tightened. Loosened No. 2 and nothing happened. Loosened No. 1 again and when tightened the noise gradually stopped. Might have been a sticky valve?*

Weather: *Hazy sun, light SE wind*

Navigation: *Departed Gosport Harbor 5:50 AM under power. Destination Jewel Island. Fog set in at 9:30 AM. P turned on radar. Fog lifted at 10:30 AM. Turned radar off. Passed Old Anthony Rock at 12:35 PM. Anchored at Jewel Island at 2:30 PM – lots of room – only four other boats. Wind stayed light all day and we motored the whole distance.*

Pearl III at Jewel Island

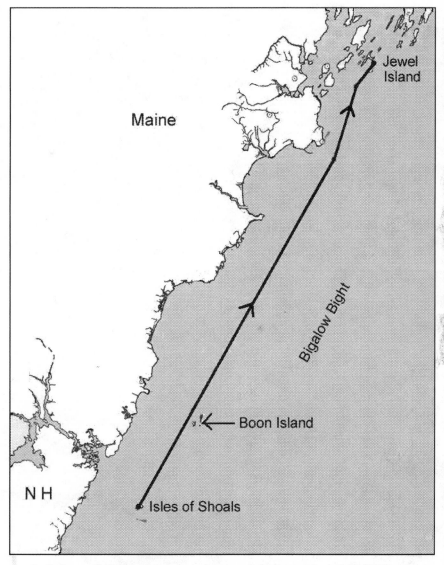

Isles of Shoals to Jewel Island - 49 Miles

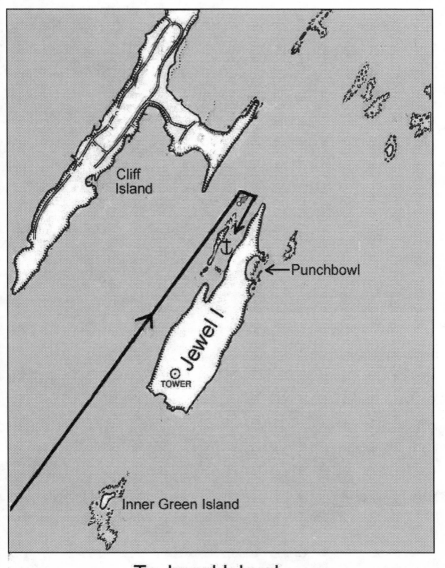

Cliff
Island

Punchbowl

Jewel I

TOWER

Inner Green Island

To Jewel Island

Boon Island Light

Boon Island was the site of a terrible shipwreck in 1710. The British *Nottingham Galley* ran onto this desolate pile of rocks in a severe northeast blizzard. The ship broke up and the crew was marooned in the bitter winter weather for 3-1/2 weeks until rescued by fishermen from the town of York, Maine. Ten members of the crew had kept themselves alive by resorting to cannibalism when their less fortunate shipmates died of exposure or starvation. For many years after this shipwreck the fisherman left a barrel of provisions on the island as a boon for shipwrecked sailors, thus the name "Boon Island". 100 years after the *Nottingham Galley* shipwreck a lighthouse was finally built on the island.

Day and Date: *Monday July 29, day 6 - Jewel Island to Christmas Cove*

Check List:

Water 1: *In use 4 days*	**Battery 1**: *12.4*
Water 2: *Full*	**Battery 2:** *12.4*
CNG 1: *Empty*	**Fuel:** *1/2+*
CNG 2: *1800 - day 1*	**Holding tank:** *Pumped*
Log: *142*	**Engine hrs:** *1692.5*

Problems: *Put on the Genoa because of the light SW wind. P lost the pin holding the tack overboard when changing sails. Had to makeshift with a smaller pin and tape around it so it won't fall out. It fell out later because not well taped. P tied the tack with 1/8" line.*

Weather: *Thick fog. Visibility 3 or 4 boat lengths. Light SW wind.*

Navigation: *Departed Jewel Island for Christmas cove at 9:40 AM under power. Sea lumpy again and boat lurching around. Put up main to try to steady it but the wind was too light. Fog persisted until Fuller Rock, where it scaled up some so visibility was about 1/2 mile. By the time we reached Christmas Cove at 2:30 PM the fog had lifted and it was a bright sunny day. Once again we motored all the way. Navigation in the fog has become a lot easier. With GPS we know exactly where we are, and with radar we can see the other boats. Buoys show up on the radar and also on the GPS "map".*

Comments: *Called Duggans in the morning before we left Jewel Island. They will join us at Christmas Cove for dinner at the Coveside Restaurant. Called them again from Christmas Cove and they arrived about 4 PM. They came out to the boat and we had crackers and cheese and drinks. Paul does not drink liquor any more, so he had a small beer. Joyce and Maria had cranapple juice, and I had a Martini. Paul sold his sailboat – said he has not been well and can't sail anymore. He has emphysema and arthritis. He hasn't been doing any bird carving for some time, but hopes to get back to it soon. Maria seems to be doing very well with Parkinson's. She climbed onto the boat from the dinghy with no trouble. They see Pete and Nancy Engels quite often, and will be driving up to Vermont to see them later this summer. We had a nice dinner – haddock and a bottle of Pinot Grigio. Blueberry pie and ice cream for dessert.*

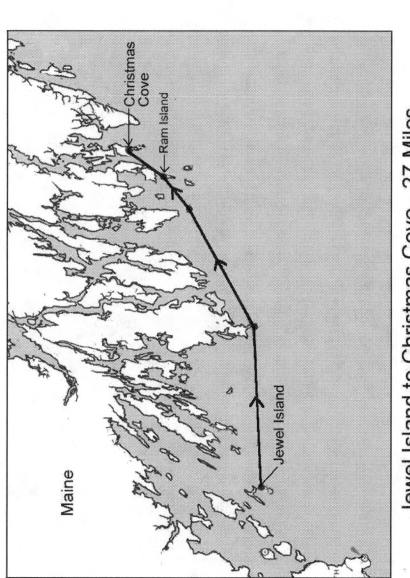

Jewel Island to Christmas Cove - 27 Miles

Ram Island Light at Fisherman Island Passage
(near Boothbay)

The first light on Ram Island was a lantern put there by a local fisherman. He had come perilously close to wrecking his boat on the Ram Island rocks when returning home after dark one evening. Following his narrow escape he set out a lantern each evening for the safety of his fellow sailors. After he moved away a dory with a lantern in its bow was anchored by the rocks. The lantern was lighted each day by the last fisherman sailing by at sunset. A lighthouse, keepers quarters, a boat house, and a launching ramp were built on Ram Island thirteen years after the fisherman's first lantern.

A raised wooden walkway from the keeper's house (on the island to the left in the photograph above) fell into disrepair and had to be demolished after the light was automated in the 1930's.

The Coveside Restaurant and Marina

Paul and Maria Duggan

Day and Date: *Tuesday July 30, day 7 - Christmas Cove to Hall and Harbor Islands*

Check List:

Water 1: *In use 5 days*   **Battery 1:** *12.4*
Water 2: *Full*   **Battery 2:** *12.6*
CNG 1: *Empty*   **Fuel:** *Filled at Coveside*
CNG 2: *1800 – day 2*   **Holding tank:** *1/4 full*
Engine hrs: *1697.7*   **Log:** *169*

Weather: *Bright sunny day at start. No wind – flat calm. Clouded up and rained in morning then cleared about 1 PM. Still no wind. Wind picked up a little from SW about 4:00 PM. Clouds and sun for the rest of the day. Relatively warm – shorts and short sleeves.*

Navigation: *Departed Christmas Cove 2:15 PM. Motored and tried sailing but not enough wind until about 4:00 PM. Put up genny with SW wind about 10 to15 degrees off the stern to starboard. Sailed the rest of the way at about four knots. Anchored at Harbor and Hall Islands at 5:20 PM behind two other boats. Not a bad spot but would have preferred farther in where the first boat is.*

Comments: *At Christmas Cove P & J started for a walk in the morning but had to return to boat because of rain. P then took umbrella, although rain had stopped, and went to store. Bought Bisquick, oatmeal, and donuts.*

Hall Island

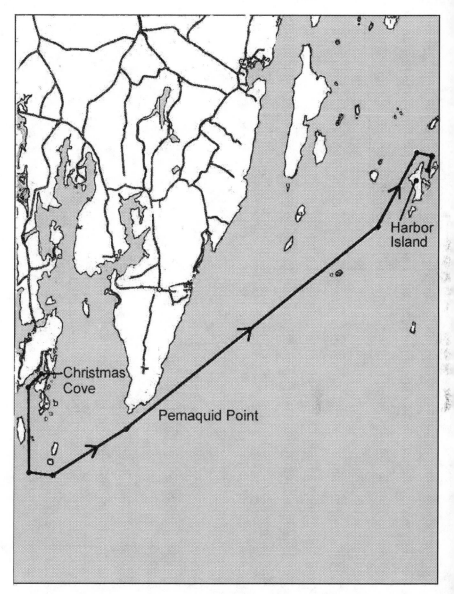

Christmas Cove to Harbor Island - 12 Miles

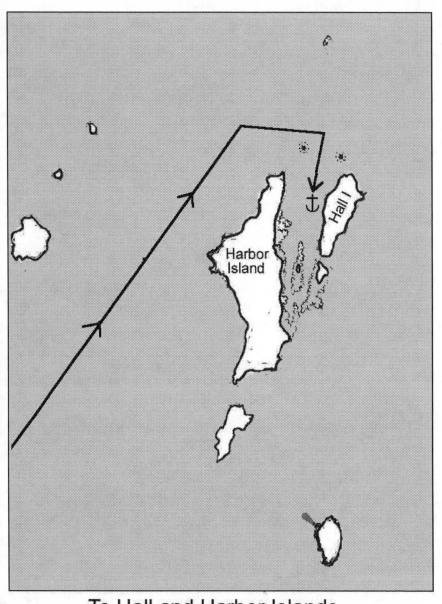

To Hall and Harbor Islands

Pemaquid Light on Pemaquid Point

Pemaquid point Lighthouse is one of the most popular spots on the Maine coast. During a typical summer about 100,00 tourists visit the site. On a nice summer day there will be dozens of people climbing around on the rocks below the lighthouse. The original lighthouse tower was built in 1828 and for many years the lighthouse keepers kept a small farm on the property to produce food and provide supplementary income.

Day and Date: *Wednesday July 31, day 8 – Hall and Harbor Islands to Tenants Harbor*

Check List:

Water 1: *Empty at 2:00 PM (5-1/2 days)*	**Battery 1:** *12.4*
Water 2: *Full - in use*	**Battery 2:** *12.4*
CNG 1: *Empty*	**Fuel:** *Full*
CNG 2: *1760 - day 3*	**Holding tank:** *1/4 full*
Log: *181*	**Engine hrs:** *1699.5*

Problems: *When we went to bed last night a lobster pot buoy was knocking against the forward part of the hull. P was able to lift the buoy and move it to the stern of the boat where it wouldn't hit the hull. When weighing anchor in the morning a lobster pot buoy and its toggle were on opposite sites of anchor rode. The line came up twisted around the anchor but finally we got free of it.*

Weather: *Bright sun, warm, wind NW 10 k*

Navigation: *Departed Hall and Harbor Islands at 11:00 AM. Sailed part way with main and mizzen (wind almost dead astern). Put up genny after Mosquito Island. Wind 10 - 15 NW. Picked up Cod End green mooring buoy ($20) in Tenants Harbor at 1:50 PM.*

Comments: *Dinner at East Wind Inn. Excellent grilled swordfish, vegetables, and red potatoes. Good salad. Walked to post office after dinner. Beautiful evening. Sat in cockpit for awhile after returning to boat.*

Tenants Harbor

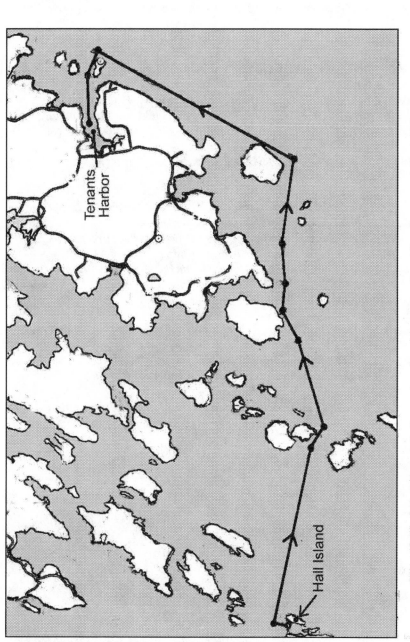

Tenants Harbor

Hall Island

Hall & Harbor Islands to Tenants Harbor -12 Miles

Day and Date: *Thursday August 1, day 9 - Tenants Harbor to Long Cove*

Check List:

Water 1: *Full (filled at Cod End)*   **Battery 1:** *12.2*
Water 2: *Full*   **Battery 2:** *12.2*
CNG 1: *Empty*   **Fuel:** *Full*
CNG 2: *1750 – day 4*   **Holding tank:** *1/4 full?*
Log: *192*   **Engine hrs:** *1700.8*

Weather: *Cloudless sky. Wind SE at 5 knots in early AM. Increased to 10 to 15 later. Warm, but cool breeze.*

Navigation: *Departed Tenants Harbor about 10:45 AM headed for Long Cove on the east side of Vinalhaven Island. Motored to Two Bush Island, then put up main and genny. Had a nice sail across West Penobscot Bay. Dropped genny and sailed up Hurricane Sound under main and mizzen to Long Cove. Two other sailboats in Long Cove, but plenty of room to anchor. Dropped anchor in 23 ft at 3:15 PM. There now are a lot of private moorings in the cove, taking up a lot of good anchoring space.*

Comments: *Took Pearl III in to Cod End float about 8:00 AM. Got water and a bag of ice cubes. We had been using ice from the trays that came with the Cold Machine, but they are a nuisance. Took 51 gallons of water. We rowed ashore later, bought groceries at the grocery store, and halibut at Cod End.*

We had halibut, pasta, and salad for dinner. P took off the ventilator in the main cabin – it was frozen and couldn't be opened and closed. Cleaned the screen, which was very dirty, but couldn't free up the adjusting screw. Soaked it with WD40 and will try tomorrow. Watched a video, "The Guns of Navarone".

Two Bush Island Light

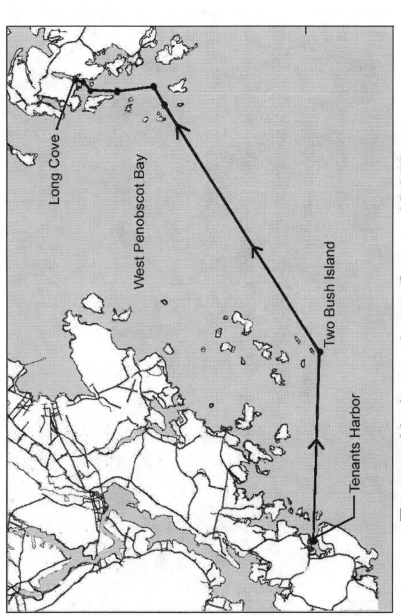

Long Cove

West Penobscot Bay

Two Bush Island

Tenants Harbor

Tenants Harbor to Long Cove - 19 Miles

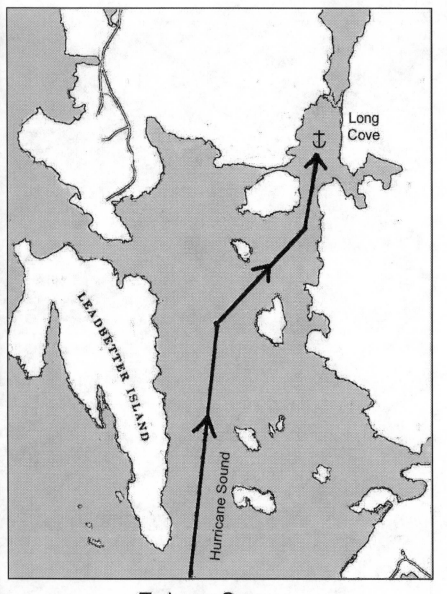

To Long Cove

Long Cove

Day and Date: *Friday August 2, day 10 - Long Cove to McGlathery Island*

Check List:

Water 1: *In use 1 day*   **Battery 1:** *12.4*
Water 2: *Full*   **Battery 2:** *12.6*
CNG 1: *Empty*   **Fuel:** *7/8 full*
CNG 2: *1500 - day 5*   **Holding tank:** *Pumped*
Log: *211*   **Engine hrs:** *1703*

Weather: *Clear and sunny. Wind S at 5 knots early, then shifted to SE at 10-15. Clouded up after we arrived at McGlathery.*

Navigation: *Departed Long Cove at 10:00 AM headed for McGlathery Island. Motored down Hurricane Sound and The Reach past the south end of Vinalhaven, then P put up sails (main, genoa, and mizzen). Sailed across East Penobscot Bay with SE wind at 12 knots, steady. Dropped genoa and motored from Merchant Island. Dropped anchor at McGlathery I. at 1:20 PM.*

Comments: *Before we left Long Cove P installed a light over the mirror in the forward cabin. It was the one from the forward end of the starboard settee. We have one at home that will replace it. When we arrived at McGlathery there were two other boats rafted together near the south end of the harbor, a "tug" and a 40' yawl. They left at 1:45 PM and we were alone! Later a Bermuda 40 came in and a small powerboat landed at the beach and stayed for the night. The weather was not nice and we did not go ashore. It is amazing how the trees have grown. The clearing where the boys tented years ago is all grown in.*

McGlathery Island Camp Site Grown In

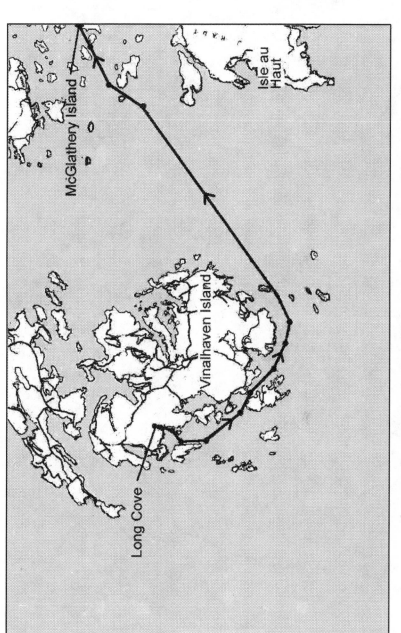

Long Cove to McGlathery Island - 17 Miles

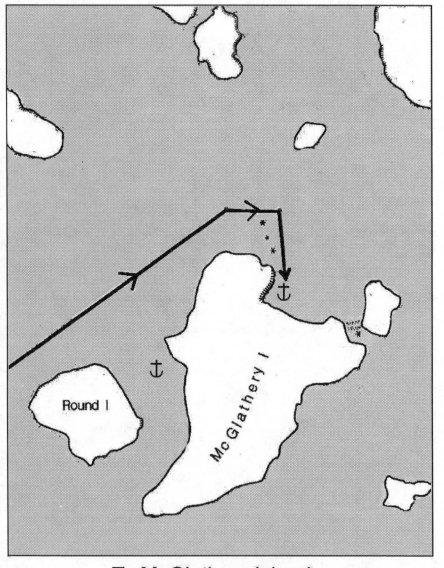

To McGlathery Island

Rocks at McGlathery Island

Day and Date: *Saturday August 3, day 11 - McGlathery Island to Lunt Harbor*

Check List:

Water 1: *In use 2 days*	**Battery 1:** *14.4*
Water2: *Full*	**Battery 2:** *14.5*
CNG 1: *Empt*	**Fuel:** *7/8*
CNG 2: *1450 - day 6*	**Holding tank:** *1/4*
Log: *228*	**Engine hrs:** *1704.9*

Weather: *Early morning fog. Wind light and variable. Fog lifted after we arrived at Lunt Harbor, and it got hot.*

Navigation: *Departed McGlathery Island at 11:00 AM headed for Long Island. Some fog. Visibility ranged from 1/2 to 1 mile. Wind less than 5 knots. Motored all the way. Arrived Lunt Harbor at 1:15 PM.*

Comments: *Rock and roll at McGlathery in the early morning when the lobster boats were going out (starting before 5:00 AM). Only other boats were a Hinckley Bermuda 40 that came in last night at about 6:00 PM, and a small powerboat that went up onto the beach and stayed there last night.*

Rowed in to the Lunt Harbor Deli. Picked up crab rolls for lunch and ordered lobsters, potato salad, cole slaw, and blueberry pie for dinner. Pick up at 6 PM. The Deli is now open from 11 AM to 8 PM. Joyce's lobster was tough! P didn't know it until too late or he would have shared his. Everything else was good, including the Lindemans Chardonnay.

The Lunt Deli

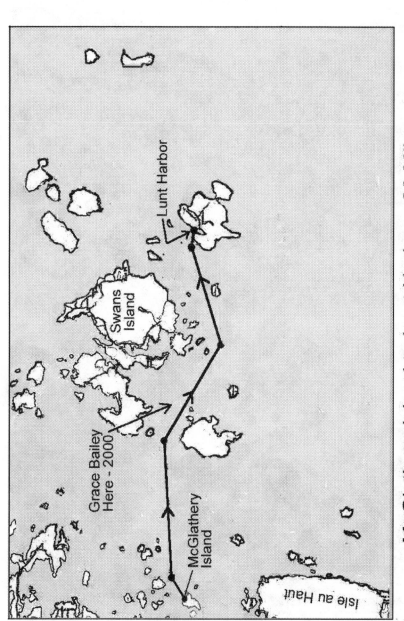

McGlathery Island to Lunt Harbor - 28 Miles

Two Views of the Back Harbor at Frenchboro

Day and Date: *Sunday August 4, day 12 - Lunt Harbor to Eastern Cove*
Check List:

Water 1: *In use 3 days*	**Battery 1:** *12.4*
Water 2: *Full*	**Battery 2:** *12.5*
CNG 1: *Empty*	**Fuel:** *3/4+*
CNG 2: *1350 - day 7*	**Holding tank:** *Pumped*
Log: *239*	**Engine hrs:** *1707.3*

Weather: *9 ᴀᴍ–Slightly overcast, light fog, no wind. Cleared up by noon. Wind turned SW 5-10 k.*

Navigation: *Motored to Eastern Cove in the morning. Tried to pick up a mooring, but the chain went through it and it was impossible. We anchored in about 30'. Saw another mooring on the west side that looked OK, but stayed anchored. Left about 3:00 and sailed back under genny and mizzen.*

Comments: *"Bagpiper" from Marion came in to Lunt Harbor as we went out. At Eastern Cove there was a lobster boat from Bass Harbor in near the beach and a large crowd on the beach having a picnic. A pleasant place on a quiet day, but the tombolo is low and does not provide much protection from a SW wind. Went ashore in Frenchboro in the afternoon and walked as far as the town dump.*

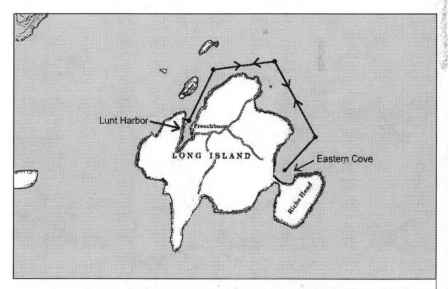

Lunt Harbor to Eastern Cove

Day and Date: *Monday August 5, day 13 - Lunt Harbor to Northeast Harbor*

Check List:

Water 1: *In use 4 days*
Water 2: *Full*
CNG 1: *Empty*
CNG 2: *1250 – day 8*
Log: *244*

Battery 1: *12.5*
Battery 2: *12.4*
Fuel: *3/4+*
Holding tank: *Empty*
Engine hrs: *1708.9*

Weather: *Rain and some light fog.*

Navigation: *Departed Lunt Harbor at 9:20 AM heading for Northeast Harbor. Sailed under genoa and mizzen for a while and then motored when the wind went dead astern. Fog set in real thick (several boat lengths). Had a problem finding bell RW "WW" in Western Way. It was moved 1/10 mile to the northeast and renamed R"4", and the nearby nun was eliminated. The new location is shown on the computer chart, but not on the GPS.*

Picked up mooring 340 in Northeast Harbor at 12:15. $20.

Comments: *Went ashore in the afternoon. Left dirty clothes at "The Shirt off your Back" to be picked up tomorrow at 4:30 PM. Then went to bookstore and bought a Spencer and a Grisham book, and to the Pine Tree Market for food. Also bought a bicycle pump for the cabin heater at the hardware store. The old one had rusted out.*

Entering Northeast Harbor

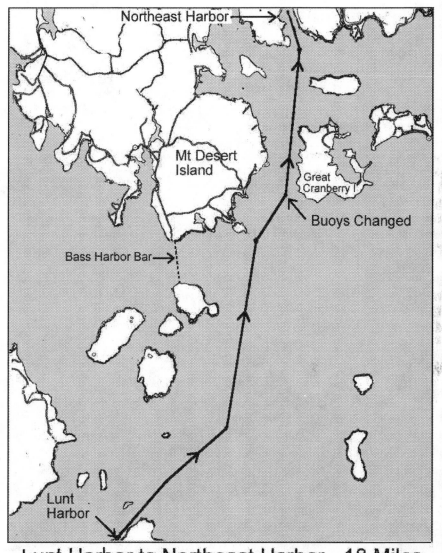

Lunt Harbor to Northeast Harbor - 18 Miles

Day and Date: *Tuesday August 6, day 14 - Northeast Harbor to Southwest Harbor and back*

Check List:

Water 1: *In use 5 days.*
Water 2: *Full*
CNG 1: *Full (new)*
CNG 2: *1100+ - day 9*
Log: *257*

Battery 1: *12.2*
Battery 2: *12.8*
Fuel: *3/4*
Holding tank: *1/2 full*
Engine hrs: *1711.7*

Weather: *Scattered clouds. Cool (65 in cabin). Wind N 15 k - picked up to 20-25 by about 10:00 AM.*

Navigation: *Motored to the Hinkley yard in Southwest Harbor for CNG. A tank plus the missing cap was $54.44! Wind had picked up to 20 to 25 knots from the north. We were able to go in to the end of the dock, which was quite a bit shorter than the boat. Filled the aft water tank. Difficult getting away from the dock because the wind was blowing in and there were boats on both sides of the dock that we had to avoid. Managed to back against the stern line and get the bow out so we could clear the boat ahead.*

Comments: *Got CNG and water at Hinkley in the AM. Showers, laundry pickup, post office, and Pine Tree Market in the afternoon (vermouth, paper towels, and balogna for sandwiches).*

Schooner at Southwest Harbor

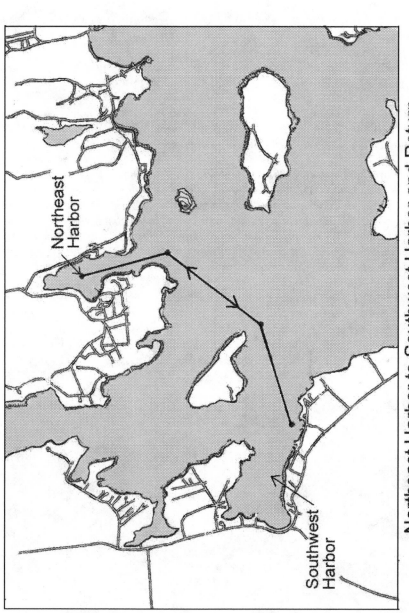

Northeast Harbor to Southwest Harbor and Return

Day and Date: *Wednesday August 7, day 15 – Northeast Harbor to Webb Cove, Hells Half Acre, & McGlathery Island*

Check List:

Water 1: *In use day 1*	**Battery 1:** *12.4*
Water 2: *Full*	**Battery 2:** *12.4*
CNG 1: *2000*	**Fuel:** *3/4*
CNG 2: *1050 - day 10*	**Holding tank:** *Empty*
Log: *262*	**Engine hrs:** *1713.1*

Weather: *Clear, sunny, and cool. 55 F in cabin. Turned on cabin heater. Wind N 5-10 knots. Picked up to 15 later then dropped again when we reached McGlathery Island. Sunny and warm at McGlathery.*

Navigation: *Departed Northeast Harbor at 9:30 AM headed for Webb Cove, which looked good for a northwest wind. Sailed a bit then wind went dead ahead and we motor-sailed with the main and mizzen. Went in to Webb Cove but it was not very attractive and there was a big ugly rusted barge about where we would have anchored. So we left and went to Hells Half Acre, but the wind was funneling through, and we went from there to McGlathery Island and anchored in the cove at 2:00 PM.. There were only two other boats, a ketch and a yawl.*

Comments: *P went ashore with bucket and clam fork at 4:00 PM. Dug for an hour or more. Not many clams, but finally got enough for chowder. The weather stayed nice and we had cocktails and read in the cockpit before dinner. More boats came in and there finally were eight of us, but most of them were far out and weren't a problem. Some rocking and rolling in the late afternoon when the lobster boats were going home.*

The Cove at McGlathery Island

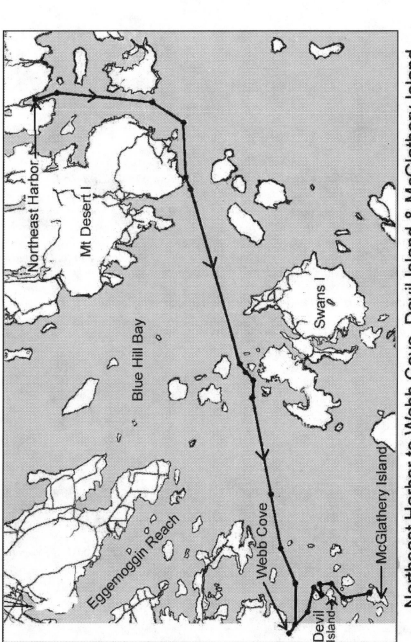

Northeast Harbor to Webb Cove, Devil Island & McGlathery Island

Day and Date: *Thursday August 8, day 16 - McGlathery Island to Seal Bay*

Check List:

Water 1: *In use 2 days*   **Battery 1:** *12.4*
Water 2: *Full*   **Battery 2:** *12.6*
CNG 1: *2000*   **Fuel:** *3/4*
CNG 2: *1050-day 11*   **Holding tank:** *1/4 full*
Log: *286*   **Engine hrs:** *1717.1*

Weather: *Sunny, light NW wind. Stayed nice all day.*

Navigation: *Departed McGlathery at 11:15 AM heading for Seal Bay. Wind light NW. Motored all the way. Dropped anchor in Seal Bay at 1:15 PM. Two other boats were in the vicinity where we anchored, but were far enough away so they were not a problem. Also a large fleet was way in at the end – looked like a club. The sailboat nearest us was from London, England. There were two couples and two small children. They were anchored over one of the rocks and had to move when the tide went down. We saw several seals in Seal Bay!*

Comments: *At McGlathery the first lobster boat woke us up at 4:00 AM. They continued until about 6:00, and then things leveled off. Made clam chowder for lunch. About 15 clams. Had lunch at Seal Bay. The clams were tough, but the chowder was good anyway.*

Cruising Club at Seal Bay

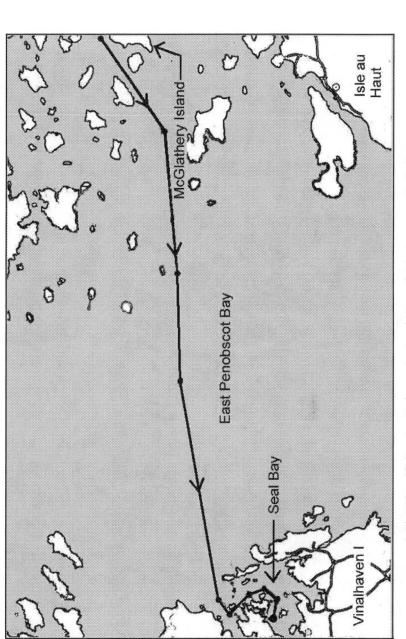

McGlathery Island to Seal Bay - 10 Miles

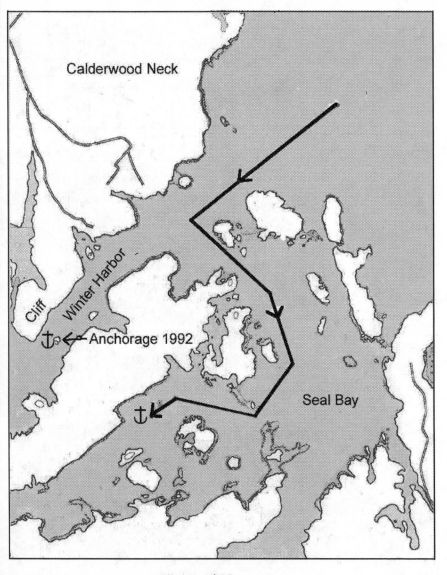

Calderwood Neck

Winter Harbor

Cliff

⚓←--- Anchorage 1992

Seal Bay

To Seal Bay

Day and date: Friday August 9, day 17 - Seal Bay to North Haven, Dix Island, and Home Harbor

Water 1: *In use 3 days*

Water 2: *Full*

CNG 1: *2000*

CNG 2: *800 - day 12*

Log: *296*

Battery 1: *12.5*

Battery 2: *12.*

Fuel: *3/4*

Holding tank: *1/2 full*

Engine hours: *1719.1*

Weather: *Bright, sunny, and cool. 55 F in cabin. Cabin heater brought it up to 70 F quickly. No wind at 7:00 AM.*

Navigation: *Left Seal Bay at 8:10 AM heading for North Haven. Motored to North Haven where we picked up a JOB mooring at 9:20. Left North Haven at 10:30 and motored to Dix and High Islands where we anchored at 1:00 PM. Not very well protected – SW wind funnels in between Dix and Birch Islands. Saw a school of porpoises on the way. Left Dix and Birch at 2:20 heading for Home Harbor. Sailed out around Little Green Island, Sunken Pond Ledge, and a lot of trash in between, then motored into the SW wind to Home Harbor, where we anchored at 3:30.*

Comments: *Rowed ashore in North Haven and went to the market. The market has moved, is much smaller, and has a lot less stuff. We bought steak, chicken, frozen stir-fry shrimp, and some other odds and ends. The windjammer Stephan Tabor was moored or anchored right next to us. We had lunch at Dix and High Islands, cocktails and steak dinner at Home Harbor. A small sailboat (about 25') came in shortly after we did, and anchored to the east and closer to the shore.*

North Haven

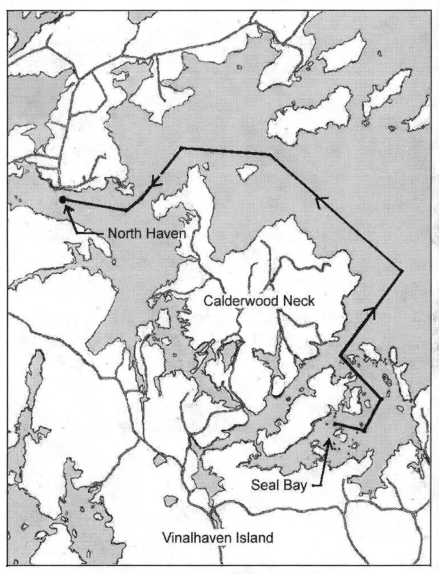

North Haven

Calderwood Neck

Seal Bay

Vinalhaven Island

Seal Bay to North Haven - 6 Miles

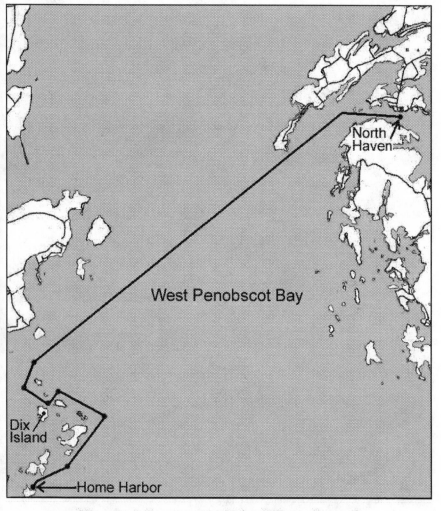

North Haven to Dix Island and
Home Harbor - 23 Miles

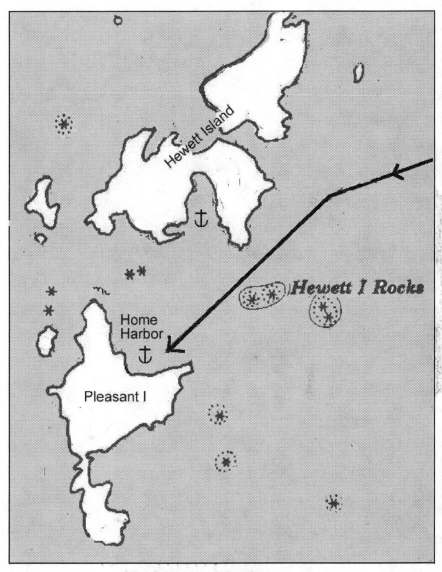

To Home Harbor

Hewett Island Rocks

Lobster Boat in Swells near Hewett Island Rocks

Day and date: Saturday August 10, day 18 - Home Harbor to Lewis Cove

Water 1: *In use 4 days*
Water 2: *Full*
CNG 1: *2000*
CNG 2: *600 – day 13*
Log: *319*

Battery 1: *12.5*
Battery 2: *12.5*
Fuel: *5/8+*
Holding tank: *Empty*
Engine hours: *1724.1*

Weather: *Scattered clouds, warm – 65 in cabin. No wind. Clouded up and wind became SW 5-10 k. Cleared up just about when we arrived at Linekin Bay.*

Navigation: *Weighed anchor in Home Harbor at 10:20 AM headed for Lewis Cove in Linekin Bay. Dropped anchor in Lewis Cove at 4:00 PM. Motored all the way.*

Comments: *Home Harbor slightly rolly at high tide, but quiet at low except for early morning when lobster boats cut through (starting at 5:00 AM).*

Problems: *Found lobster pot warp with buoy and toggle wrapped around anchor rode when weighing anchor at Home Harbor. Had a problem getting it untangled.*

Lewis Cove

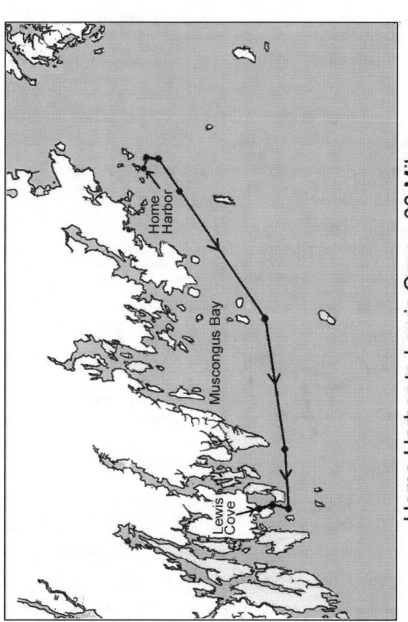

Home Harbor to Lewis Cove - 30 Miles

Day and date: Sunday August 11, day 19 - Lewis Cove to Jewel Island

Water 1: *In use 5 days*
Water 2: *Full*
CNG 1: *2000*
CNG 2: *500 – day 14*
Log: *349*

Battery 1: *12.5*
Battery 2: *12.5*
Fuel: *9/16 full*
Holding tank: *1/3*
Engine hours: *1729.8*

Weather: *Bright and sunny. No wind at 7:00 AM. SW to SSW later. Stayed nice and sunny all day.*

Navigation: *Weighed anchor at 8:20 AM. Wind picked up a little from SW mid morning. Wind up to about 10k from SSW and we sailed the last 8 miles to Jewel Island. Dropped anchor at 1:40 PM. Full of little powerboats (out for the afternoon?) and a few sailboats.*

Comments: *A small white Bayliner (ugh) named "Eagle Sea" anchored beside us about an hour after we arrived. P noticed that the anchor rode was almost straight up and down. Some time later it had moved back, but we saw no one aboard. Then later it was farther back, obviously dragging its anchor and heading for the reef at the north side of the entrance to the harbor. A small Maine power boat (about 20' long and shaped like a lobster boat) came in and P hailed him and explained what was happening. He said, "Hop aboard and we'll go get it". We did, and as we were pulling up the anchor a woman stuck her head out of the forward hatch. Her husband, kids, and another couple had gone ashore and she had been asleep. She was scared silly and kept saying, "I don't know what to do!" We towed the boat back to where it had started, let out more scope, and dropped the anchor. When the shore crew returned and they were leaving P told the man he didn't have enough scope out. He said he had let out a lot of rope and some chain!*

Most powerboats left late afternoon. There were about a dozen boats overnight, mostly sailboats and one big trawler from New Brunswick.

The Cuckolds

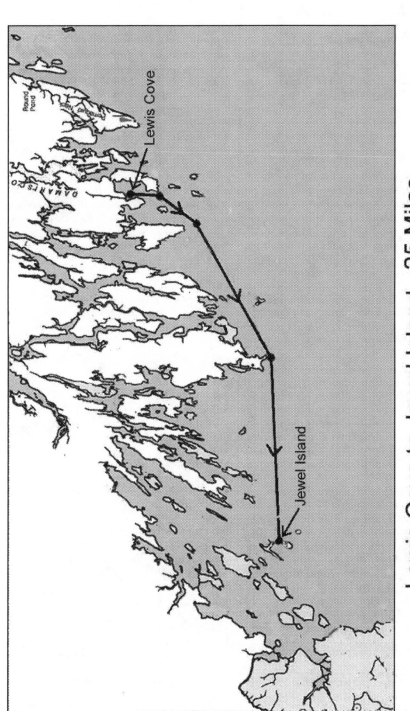

Lewis Cove to Jewel Island - 25 Miles

Day and date: Monday August 12, day 20 - Jewel Island to Isles of Shoals

Water 1: *Empty*   **Battery 1:** *12.5*
Water 2: *full*   **Battery 2:** *12*
CNG 1: *2000*   **Fuel:** *1/2+*
CNG 2: *350 – day 15*   **Holding tank:** *5/8 full*
Log: *374*   **Engine hours:** *1733.4*

Weather: *Clear and windless at 6:00 AM.*

Navigation: *Weighed anchor at Jewel Island at 7:00 AM. No wind at start. Wind gradually picked up from SW. Sea very lumpy. Some fog off and on. Motored until 2:00 PM when wind veered to S at 10-15 knots. Sailed the last 10 miles (2 hours). Picked up red ball mooring in Gosport Harbor at 4:00 PM. There were not many boats and a lot of empty moorings. More boats came in during the afternoon, but there was still plenty of room. Not like our last trip!*

Problems: *Starter refused to operate after genoa was taken down. After multiple pushes of the switches it finally caught. Don't know what the problem was.*

The Oceanic Hotel on Star Island at the Isles of Shoals

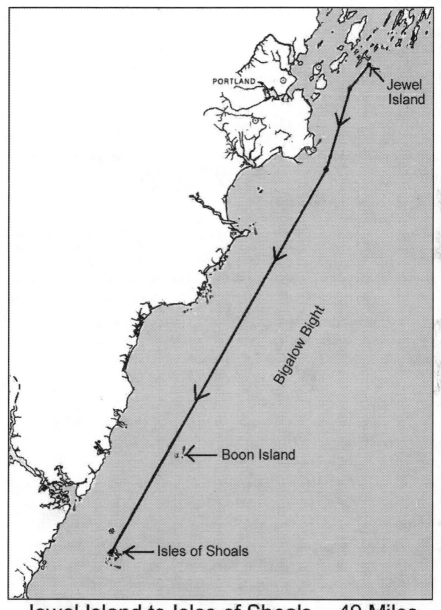

Jewel Island to Isles of Shoals - 49 Miles

Day and date: Tuesday August 13, day 21 - Isles of Shoals to Scituate

Water 1: *Empty*   **Battery 1:** *12.4*
Water 2: *Full. In use.*   **Battery 2:** *12.4*
CNG 1: *2000*   **Fuel:** *1/2-*
CNG 2: *200 – day 16*   **Holding tank:** *1/4*
Log: *424*   **Engine hours:** *1740*

Weather: *Hazy sun with light SW wind at 6:30 AM.*

Navigation: *Left Gosport Harbor at 7:00 AM bound for Scituate. Motored for a while, then wind came up from SW and we sailed for a while. After Cape Ann we motored a while, then there was a wind shift to SSE. We sailed to the east of Minots Light and then motored the last 5 miles. Wind got as high as 18 knots, but boat was fine with reefed genny, main, and mizzen. Arrived in Scituate about 4:40 and got a mooring from Easy Rider.*

Comments: *Took trash ashore, had dinner at the Mill Wharf Restaurant, and went to the grocery store. In the restaurant P overheard the man at the next table mentioning the names "Morehouse", "Thomas", "Dick", and "Peter". P thought it must be Jack Chesley, so before dessert P got up and spoke to him. It <u>was</u> Jack Chesley and we had a long talk with him and the couple he was with. He is retired and lives in Scituate. The last time we saw Jack was in Maine 28 years ago. The other man is a retired urologist and lives in Hingham. He was at the Mary Fletcher Hospital, and they have three children they adopted from the Lund home, where we got Tim. Dick Morehouse is on Vinalhaven for the summer. He is in his eighties and is still working – on three projects!*

Fishing Boat in Bigelow Bight

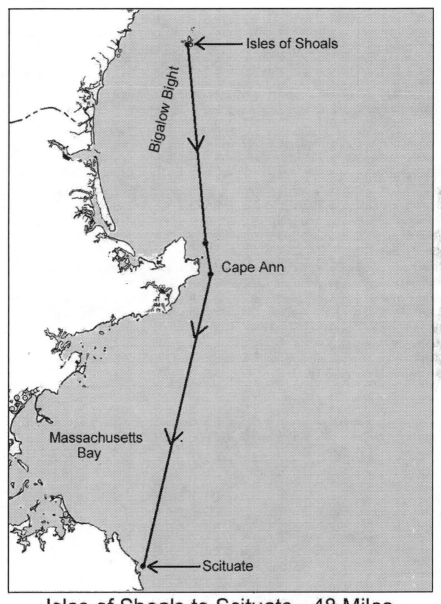

Isles of Shoals

Bigalow Bight

Cape Ann

Massachusetts
Bay

Scituate

Isles of Shoals to Scituate - 48 Miles

Day and date: Wednesday August 14, day 22 - Scituate to Bassetts Island

Water 1: *full*

Water 2: *Full*

CNG 1: *2000*

CNG 2: *Empty – 16.5 days*

Log: *478*

Battery 1: *12.4*

Battery 2: *12.4*

Fuel: *Full (+28 gs @ Scituate)*

Holding tank: *1/4 full*

Engine hours: *1748?*

Weather: *Sunny and warm. 70+ in cabin at 8:00 AM. Record heat forecast. SW wind 5-10 knots at start, then picked up.*

Navigation: *Left Scituate at 8:30 AM after filling diesel tank and water tanks. Sailed and motor sailed off and on to Farnum Rock – arrived at 10:25. Wind shifted to south at Farnum Rock and then we motored. At about 11:00 we were almost run down by a large powerboat approaching from our port side on a collision course. They refused to change course or speed, although we had the right of way, and we had to turn out of the way at the last minute and face the waves. About five miles from the canal the wind piped up to 18-20 knots. Current in the canal was supposed to be 0.2 knots against us, but it turned out to be 2 knots. Wind was 15-20 on the nose through the canal, and the current didn't turn in our favor until we got to the RR Bridge. Wind in Hog Island Channel was SW at 18-20 knots and the hobbyhorses became atrocious. Several times the bow was buried, and at times we were only doing 2 knots with the engine running at 2000 RPM! When we could we turned south out of the channel and headed for Bassetts Island. Picked up the RBHYC mooring at about 4:30 PM. All in all a pretty crazy day. All the wind we didn't have for 3 weeks accumulated and let us have it in the last few hours.*

Breakwater Light – East End of Cape Cod Canal

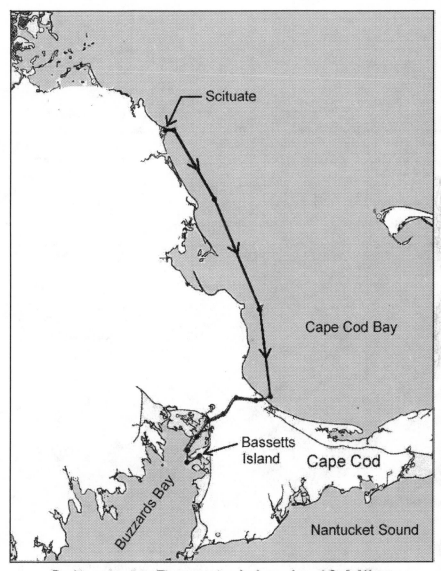

Scituate

Cape Cod Bay

Bassetts
Island

Cape Cod

Buzzards Bay

Nantucket Sound

Scituate to Bassets Island - 43 Miles

Day and date: Thursday August 15, day 23 - Bassetts Island to Marion

Water 1: *In use 1 day*
Water 2: *Full*
CNG 1: *2000*
CNG 2: *Empty*
Log: *528 at Marion*

Battery 1: *12.4*
Battery 2: *12.3*
Fuel: *3/4+*
Holding tank: *Empty*
Engine hours: *1755.6*

Weather: *Overcast, warm (75 in cabin at 7:00 AM). Wind SW around 10 knots in harbor.*

Navigation: *Left Bassetts at 8:30 AM. Sailed with reefed main and stays'l. Wind 15-20 SW. Motor sailed part of the way when the waves began to slow us. Made it past Bird Island without tacking. From Bird Island the wind was on the beam and we were doing better than 6 knots with reefed main and stays'l! Arrived at town dock at 10:15.*

Comments: *Had a nice sail from Bassetts Island to Marion. A good ending to a successful cruise. Head pumped at town dock.*

Bird Island Light

This tiny spit of land once was the site of a lighthouse tower, a stone keeper's house, a barn, a boathouse, a landing pier, fences, and a 280' sea wall. All but the lighthouse tower and keeper's house were demolished by a storm in 1869. The keeper's house was taken down in 1890. Some of the structures were rebuilt, but were destroyed by the great 1938 hurricane.

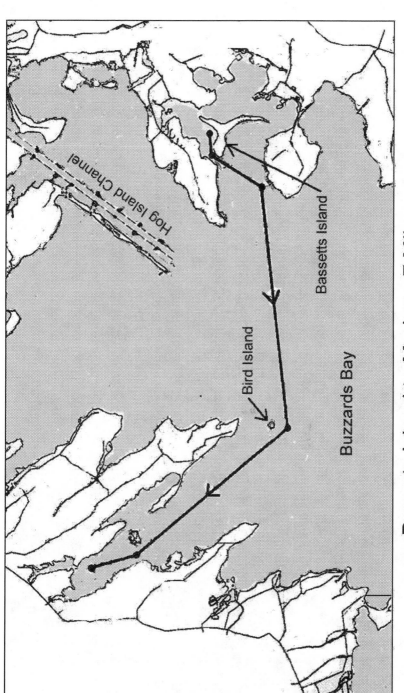

Hog Island Channel

Bassetts Island

Bird Island

Buzzards Bay

Bassets Island to Marion - 7 Miles

23
THE LAST MAINE CRUISE

The start of the Maine cruise in August 2003 was not an auspicious one. We left the mooring and halfway out of the harbor I lost the jib halyard up the mast. We motored to the town float and two men were there. One of them volunteered to hoist me up the mast in my bosn's chair, and I retrieved the halyard. We motored through the canal and had a beautiful sail up the coast to Scituate. It was a bright sunny day with a steady southwest wind. At Scituate we got a mooring from Easy Rider and stayed for the night.

In the morning there was thick fog and no wind. We had all the navigation equipment required to sail in limited visibility: radar, GPS, a laptop computer that we could plot courses on charts and transfer them to the GPS, and a good depth sounder (I had replaced the faulty Signet with a reliable Autohelm unit). So we ignored the fog and headed for Jewel Island.

We passed Thatcher Island off Cape Ann on our way to Jewel Island. The lighthouses were visible in the fog.

Thatcher Island

For 11 straight days we navigated in the fog. Several afternoons it lifted briefly but then closed in again. Natives that we talked to said they had never seen anything like it in all their lives. We went to places we had been before except for one new anchorage at Cow Island at the northern part of Muscongus Bay. It was highly recommended by Taft and Taft as a beautiful spot.

When we arrived at Cow Island the fog was so thick that all we saw of it was a dim blur. Just as we were anchoring there was a great crash. The gooseneck holding the boom to the mast had broken and the forward end of the boom had crashed down on the cabin top. The boom for the roller-furling mainsail was extremely heavy since it had to be large enough to hold the rolled-up sail. I inspected the gooseneck and found that it could be repaired by welding the break, and if properly done would be better than new. The best place for having this done would be Rockland, so that would be our destination in the morning.

We motored 28 miles to Rockland the next day in the fog. The Northend Shipyard sounded like a good bet to get the gooseneck welded so I went to what I thought was their float – there was no sign. I went into the building to inquire and was told that I was at the Schooner Wharf, and that the shipyard was the next float, which was 15 or 20 yards away. So I went back to the boat to motor over to the Northend Shipyard float, which brought up another problem – the starter wouldn't work and I couldn't start the engine. I took the broken gooseneck and rowed over to the shipyard float, went in, and explained my two problems to the mechanic. He said he would send the fitting out to be welded and it should be back sometime in the afternoon. I then rowed a line over to *Pearl III* and we pulled her over to the shipyard float and worked on the starter. Eventually we discovered that there was a bad connection between the starter button and the starter relay. It was resolved by installing a new wire. The repaired gooseneck came in the afternoon, I installed it, attached the boom, and everything was back in order.

We left Rockport in the fog with the intention of treating ourselves to drinks and a nice dinner at the Sail Loft in Rockland.. To our dismay, when we got there we found that the restaurant was closed and another business had taken over the space. This was the third minor disaster in a row and a big disappointment – we had enjoyed the ambience and the food and drinks at the Sail Loft.

Another place visited was McGlathery Island. It was foggy there, as it was everywhere else, but it was quiet and peaceful and there was no wind. It was pleasant enough to enjoy a drink in the cockpit under the awning before going below for dinner.

McGlathery Island in the Fog

Looking in to Christmas Cove

We got to Christmas Cove and had drinks and dinner at the Coveside Restaurant as usual. It was foggy there.

We went to Lunt Harbor and to the Lunt Deli for lobsters to take back to the boat. It was foggy there.

Lunt Harbor at Long Island

The Lunt Deli

Pearl III anchored in the fog

Fog didn't keep the Outward Bound boats in Harbor

Schooner in the fog

Buoy in the fog

Other boats in the Fog

In spite of the extended period of fog during our 2003 Maine cruise we enjoyed ourselves as we did on all our cruises, fair weather or foul.

During this cruise the Charles River Sail and Power Squadron (renamed by adding Sail) held a rendezvous far up the New Meadows River at a location I thought was inappropriate because the water was too shallow for the sailboats of most members. Never-the-less we made arrangements with Jerry and Ann Schwarzkopf to meet them at Sebasco Harbor Resort and drive with them to the Rendezvous. They stayed overnight with us on *Pearl III*. At the rendezvous we had a clambake and an auction, both of which had become standard features of the rendezvous. For the auction, squadron members contributed nautical items they no longer needed or wanted. We contributed a folding bicycle – Joyce no longer was riding hers. Although I had folded and unfolded them many times I had a lot of difficulty unfolding the one that was for sale, after telling the gathering how easy it was. The fog had lifted before the rendezvous.

Sebasco Harbor Resort

One of our stops on the way back to Marion was Jewel Island. As usual we were returning on a weekend, so the popular places were crowded. We arrived at Jewel Island early enough that we had no trouble finding a place to anchor but it was all downhill from there. The fog had lifted several days before and the weather was bright and sunny. Jewel Island was a different place from the one we often had stopped at on our way to and from Maine. After we anchored the cove became crowded with boats of all sizes and descriptions, including many small powerboats. There were tents and campsites ashore, the shore was littered with people getting into and out of dinghies, and there were crowds of people on some of the anchored boats. It was not a peaceful, secluded spot like it was when John and I first visited on *Snoopy* in 1972

Jewel Island on a 2003 Weekend

We did a lot of thinking following the 2003 Maine Cruise. We were in our late seventies, pushing eighty. I was starting to make more mistakes than usual; Joyce had stopped riding the folding bike and was beginning to have difficulty getting aboard, even using the folding step I had made; and we had been to most of the harbors and anchorages in Maine that we wanted to see (been there, done that) and many of them were now crowded with boats and noisy people. In addition, I was getting tired of all the time I was spending getting *Pearl III* ready in the spring. I always wanted her to look like new inside and out, and this was getting more difficult – *Pearl* III was aging as we were. The work included: cleaning and polishing the topsides and all the other fiberglass; treating (and sometimes sanding) the teak caprail, main hatch, hatch boards, and cockpit coaming; sanding and painting the bottom every few years; installing and removing the cover frame and the covers; changing the oil in the motor; draining the water tanks and adding anti-freeze; packing up the remaining food, bedding, and clothes and taking them home; and numerous other tasks. With regrets we decided it was time to "swallow the anchor" and sell *Pearl III*.

In the spring of 2004 we put *Pearl III* on the market. In the middle of the summer we had a good offer from a fellow from Harwich Massachusetts who was working in Australia. He wanted to buy the boat and sail it to Australia and he made a deposit of $11,000. The Crealock 37 was a blue water boat that had successfully competed in the Transpac race across the Pacific, so sailing to Australia was not a far-fetched idea. The day we were going to complete the transaction we drove to the broker's office in Marion and waited for the buyer to show up. While we were waiting the broker received an email – the buyer couldn't go through with the purchase and would forfeit his deposit. Half went to the broker and half to us.

Late the next summer we received another acceptable offer, this time from a couple in England. The man's father had a Crealock 37 yawl and he wanted one just like it. I was sure we had him hooked. Most Crealock 37's were sloops – very few yawls had been built. The sale went through. When the boat was launched the next spring I went aboard to go over it with them and explain about the various changes I had made. I asked them if they would be sailing the boat back to England and to my surprise they said "No". They had rented a slip in Greenwich, Connecticut and they would be leaving it there. I thought 70 miles was a long commute from Lexington to Marion, but 3,000 miles from England to Connecticut!

Thus ended almost 70 years of messing around with boats of one kind or another.

24
THE DINGHIES

Although there is some information about our dinghies in other chapters of this book, dinghies are so important to cruising sailboats that they deserve a separate chapter. During our sailing years we had a total of six dinghies. I designed and made four of them and we bought the other two. They all had advantages and disadvantages. No dinghy is perfect.

I made small models (one-half inch to the foot) out of heavy paper for all the dinghies I designed and built. They all were made of plywood using the "stitch and glue" method. Using this method the pieces are cut out of sheets of plywood, fastened together with copper wire inserted from the inside through holes about 4" apart in adjacent pieces, then twisted on the outside to pull the pieces tightly together. The next step is to seal all the joints on the inside with 2" fiberglass tape and resin. When the resin has set the twisted wires on the outside are cut off and the joints are sealed on the outside with fiberglass tape and resin. This makes rigid watertight joints between all the pieces. The completed dinghy is then varnished or painted and the rubrail, oarlock fittings, and bow fitting for the painter are installed.

As mentioned in chapter two, after we bought the Alacrity, our "pocket cruiser", I designed and built our first dinghy. I made several small models of stiff paper and used them to lay out full-size patterns. Bolt Beranek and Newman, where I worked, had a model shop that the employees were allowed to use for personal projects. I went across the street to the Continental Can Company Cardboard Warehouse and got several 4ft by 8ft sheets of corrugated cardboard, cut out the patterns, and taped them together with duct tape. When the full-size model was completed John Brennan, the maintenance man, looked at it and said, "Parker, you're gonna drown".

Small Model of Dinghy No.1

The completed dinghy was made of 1/8" marine plywood for light weight so I could easily carry it and haul it on board when necessary. The design was somewhat complicated in order to achieve adequate stiffness and stability. The complications included a double-V bottom and a partial deck. It turned out to be very stable and rowed well. It also towed well, even at high speeds. We named it *Nit 1* when we bought *Pearl II*. I rigged *Nit* 1 for sailing, and although the hull shape was not ideal for sailing, our son John and I enjoyed sailing it. *Nit 1* was lost while being towed in a storm when we were returning from Maine in 1981 (see page 87).

Nit 1 with Double V Bottom   *Nit 1* Towing at High Speed

Dinghy No.2 was meant to be a temporary replacement for dinghy No.1 after we lost it in Maine. It was made of a single 4ft by 8ft sheet of 1/4" exterior-grade plywood just to get me back and forth to the boat at the mooring. I made it quickly using the same stitch and glue method I had used on No.1. The design proved to be totally impractical. It was so narrow that when I tried it out the first time it almost capsized and dumped me into Marion Harbor. To prevent this I had to sit on the bottom, which made it almost impossible to row. I used it for just one trip from the dock to *Pearl II* and back. Then it was back to the drawing board. It might have been a good dinghy for a small child.

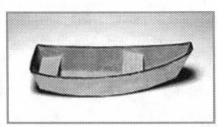 

Model of Dinghy No.2   Model of Dinghy No.3

Dinghy No.3 was made by sawing No.2 down the middle and adding a 10" wide seat extending from bow to stern, with the space between the seat and the bottom filled with polystyrene floatation. Like *Nit 1* it had a partial deck for stiffness. Dinghy No.3 proved to be stable, towed well, and rowed well. The longitudinal seat (see page 101) allowed variable seating locations for balancing the boat. No.3 was destroyed when it flew off the roof of the car and smashed bow first into a utility pole (see page 104).

Rowing Dinghy No.3

After No.3 was destroyed we bought No.4, the Perrywinkle, named after its designer Robert Perry. This was a beautiful dinghy made of fiberglass and trimmed with a lot of teak: floor boards, caprails, and gratings on seats. It had a canoe stern and the design went well with the design of *Pearl III*. It rowed well and sailed beautifully. There were several negatives – it was difficult to carry and hoist on deck because of its weight, and

Dinghy No.4, the Perrywinkle

it towed poorly at high sailing speeds. At six knots the stern squatted, and at seven knots it squatted so much that water was sucked in over the stern. In addition it had a round bottom and therefore was not as stable as dinghy

No.1 with its double V bottom or No.3 with its flat bottom. We sometimes used a 1-1/2 horsepower air-cooled Cruise and Carry outboard motor on the Perrywinkle.

Dinghy No.5 was an Avon inflatable that could be rolled up and stored in a cockpit locker for offshore passages, then inflated when we reached our destination. This eliminated the need to hoist the Perrywinkle on board and lash it down on deck (I was getting lazier as time went on). Like all inflatables it was extremely stable – you could stand on a side tube without tipping it over. We often used a 3-1/2 horsepower outboard motor on the Avon because it rowed so poorly..

The plywood floorboards for the Avon were ordered separately and didn't arrive until a week after the dinghy. Our trip without floorboards was interesting. We loaded our gear, which was in boat bags, into the Avon and then stepped in. The floor went down where we stepped and the boat bags tumbled into us in a heap. Without floorboards the Avon is impractical.

There were two plywood floorboards connected in the middle. I made some stiffeners to prevent them from depressing at the joint so they acted like a single unit. With this arrangement I found that I sometimes could bring the Avon to a plane much like an inflatable sport boat

Avon at McGlathery Island   Model of Dinghy No.6

We didn't leave our dinghies at Barden's float during the week like many people did, so the process of inflating and deflating the Avon each weekend became a real nuisance, even though I found a way to do most of the inflating with a portable vacuum cleaner.

I made dinghy No.6 to avoid the nuisance of inflating and deflating the Avon. It was made to stay on *Pearl III* on davits. Like dinghy No. 3 it had a longitudinal seat, but the seat widened near the bow and stern where it was fastened to the sides, providing stiffness to the hull. We used Barden's launch to get to and from *Pearl III* on weekends, and always had dinghy No.6 to get ashore if needed. The Avon was used for longer cruises or for long weekends when we knew we would be going ashore frequently. Because of its small size dinghy No.6 was not as stable as some of our other dinghies, but it was OK. After making the davits for No.6 I found that I could carry the Avon on the davits, which we did on our Maine cruises. We didn't leave it on the davits for long periods of time when we weren't aboard because it would fill up with rainwater (dinghy No.6 had a drain plug to avoid this problem).

Dinghy No. 6 on Davits

Avon on Davits

I rigged two of our dinghies for sailing – *Nit 1* and the Perrywinkle. To rig *Nit 1* I had to put in a centerboard well, which was the most difficult part of the job, then make and install a centerboard and rudder. Before buying a sail I made a temporary sail of polyethylene and installed a temporary mast and the rest of the rigging. It worked reasonable well and I went ahead and bought a used dinghy sail and fabricated a mast and boom. It was not the fastest sailing dinghy in the harbor but it was fun for John and me anyway.

Nit 1 with Temporary Sail and with Final Sailing Rig

Rigging the Perrywinkle was somewhat easier since it was designed as a sailing dinghy. It had a centerboard well and a socket in the forward thwart for a mast. I followed the design of the centerboard and rudder shown on a drawing of the boat, so they were the same as Robert Perry had designed them. I used a telescoping whisker pole for a mast so it was easy to stow on *Pearl III. The Perrywinkle* sailed beautifully.

John Sailing the Perrywinkle

INDEX

INDEX
(All locations are in Maine except as noted)